OPTIONS TRADING FOR BEGINNERS

2021

David Matthews

Table of Contents

Introduction

If this is the first time you've read about options trading, then sit back and relax. This is an introduction to the world of options trading. In particular, you will find that options trading is based on logic and common sense. By using these elements, you can be successful at making money right from the start.

But first, let's talk about what options are. In essence, options are contracts that two parties make to buy and sell an asset. Now, the term "asset" refers to the object that is traded. This is important to note as the asset in question could be anything. Of course, we're talking about "financial assets." As such, there is a specific number of items at play.

Specifically, stocks are at play in options trading. When you buy and sell stocks, you do so at their current market price. So, if you want to buy or sell a stock on March 15th, you will pay the price of that stock on March 15th.

But what if you could buy or sell the stock on June 10th at March 15th's price?

This is what options are all about.

Options contracts give you the flexibility to negotiate terms and conditions based on any number of parameters. These parameters will determine the nature of the contract. Consequently, you'll have the opportunity to make a profit by taking advantage of these conditions.

It is also worth noting that options contracts provide you with the opportunity to protect yourself against the risk that comes with trading in the stock market. Since the future is uncertain, options give you the chance to protect yourself from any scenario that might unfold. Therefore, options are known to "hedge" against risk. In other words, options help you protect your investments in case things take an unexpected turn.

How Options Work

The way options contracts work is quite straightforward. The two parties that engage in the negotiation agree on the price and timeframe in which stocks are bought or sold. Hence, one party agrees to sell while the other party agrees to purchase.

Now, the reason why they are "options" is because none of the parties are obligated to go through with the deal. Therefore, the buyer or seller has the "option" to go through with the contract. Otherwise, they can let the contract expire without it being used.

Based on this concept, we can infer there are two important parameters, time and price. The time parameter refers to the duration of the agreement. Options contracts can range from a few hours to months. There is no fixed timeframe for options. The time parameter can be set to any time the buyer of the contract sees fit.

The price parameter is the price at which both parties agree to conduct the deal. This is called the "strike price." As such, a strike price refers to the price point at which the buyer and seller agree to make the deal happen. As a result, if the deal is executed, the transaction will occur at the specified price. Moreover, fluctuations in market valuation are meaningless. This implies that whatever the agreed price is, that's what the contract will be based upon.

Also, please note that the buyer of the contract has the option to go through with it or not. When we say the "buyer" of the contract, we're talking about the person who holds the right to the contract. Whether the contract is to buy, or sell is irrelevant. What matters here is the individual who holds the right to the contact itself. This concept means that the contract holder can own the right to buy or sell the stock in question.

If the contract holder chooses to exercise it, the transaction will occur at the specified price point. If the contract holder chooses not to exercise it, they can let the contract expired unutilized. Therefore, the contract expires worthless, that is, with no monetary value attached to it.

Let's take a look at a practical example to highlight the concept of an options contract.

Two parties enter a negotiation. The item in question is a diamond ring. At present, the ring is worth $1,000. The ring's owner is interested in selling it. The other party is interested in buying it at a specified price point. In fact, the buyer would be willing to buy it at a cheaper price point, that is, under $1,000. So, the prospective buyer approaches the ring's owner with a proposition.

The potential buyer will purchase the ring at $900 in one month. To seal the deal, both parties enter an options contract. In this arrangement, the potential buyer purchases the contract. The buyer stipulates the conditions while the seller accepts. Under these terms, the ring's owner cannot sell it until after a month. Now, the seller could offer it around and even make deals, but they cannot sell it until the contract expires.

Let's assume that the ring's value shoots up to $1,500 after a couple of weeks. Thus, the buyer sees an opportunity and decides to execute the contract. The ring's owner cannot hike the price of the buyer. After all, that's why the contract was signed.

In this example, the buyer stands to profit as they bought the ring for a price lower than its current market valuation. The buyer could now turn around and sell the ring for a significant profit. By the same token, the seller loses out on the deal as they could have sold it at a higher price point. Yet, they could not do so unless the buyer chose to let the contract expire.

Now, let's assume that the ring's price falls to $850. At this price point, it doesn't make sense for the buyer to purchase the ring at a higher price point. So, the buyer could simply let the contract expire unused.

In this example, the buyer, as the contract holder, can choose to do let the contract go unexercised. The buyer doesn't lose anything except for the premium paid on the contract.

The premium on an options contract is charge by the writer of the contract. The writer is the person who drafts the contract, thereby becoming the counterparty to the contract holder. In this example, the ring's owner would be the writer as they are the one who has to deliver the asset in question. If the contract holder chooses to allow the contract to expire, the writer (seller in this example) makes money as they collected a fee for writing the contract. As such, the only money the buyer would lose is the premium. Please bear in mind that premiums don't have a set point. Premiums can be as low as a few pennies on the dollar value of an asset while climbing to several dollars. This is why the first thing that options traders need to become familiar with is the cost of premiums.

Chapter 1: The Right Mindset to Approach Trading

Now we need to spend some time looking at the right mindset that you need to have to trade-in options. If your mind is in the wrong place, where you don't fully understand the risks and opportunities you are taking, it will make it hard to see profits. You need to be ready to take on the market and understand what is going on because options trading can be harder to work with than others. If you can keep your mind in the game, avoid letting your emotions take over, and come up with a good strategy along the way, you will find that it is a lot easier to see results with your trading.

Trading is more of a mental game than anything else. The best tactic or the technical indicators is going to be useful to help you spot a good way into the market. But they will be worthless if you do not bring in the right mental approach to the game. It all starts before you ever place any of your trades.

Being mindful the whole time you are in the trades, and even before you enter the trades, will keep your mind clear of any emotions that may get in the way. If you are a bit worried about how this will work and whether you are smart enough to go through these trades, there are a few simple questions that you need to ask yourself before you ever consider working with options contracts. The three main questions that you should consider include:

Why am I Making this Trade?

When we get started with trading, no matter what kind of trading, there are a ton of strategies that you can use to make this successful. Things like price action and the fundamentals of the market can be enough to make anyone feel overwhelmed in no time. This is completely normal no matter who you are. No matter what tools we want to use, we have to make sure we remember why we got into the trade to start with, and then make sure you stick with these tools and only make trades that fit with your strategy.

Let's take a look at an example of how to make this happen. If you want to trade using the strategy known as moving average crossovers, you have to look at the charts and tools you have and see if any averages are crossing. If you want to trade options when there are periods with a lot more volatility, it is IV at a level that seems to make the most sense. There are a ton of strategies, and you can pick out the ones you like most. No matter which one you go with though, you have to make sure that you only place trades based on objective information. Never make a trade just to be in the market. Only be in the market and make a trade when it looks like it will make you money.

How much will I Risk on the Trade?

Risk management will be one of the most important things that you need to consider no matter what kind of investment you choose to work with.

Before choosing to place any trade, you need to figure out how much you are willing to risk on that trade. Knowing this risk from the beginning will make it easier to maintain objectivity during the trade, especially if it ends up not going the way you want. Never get into options or any kind of trade without really knowing about the risks.

Each trade should have a minimal amount of risk. The only way you can eliminate the risk is to make sure that you never enter the market. But the best way to lose all of your money is to take all that is in your account towards one trade without saving some back. Neither of these is good risk management strategies, so we need to find something that is a little bit better.

A good idea is to figure out what percentage of your account you are willing to risk each trade. It is best to stay under ten percent as a beginner. As your account starts to grow more, you may want to consider going with maybe three to five percent. You won't be able to put as much money towards the trades you do, but it can help you avoid risking too much and ending up with nothing to work with any longer.

When you keep your risk down to only ten percent, and sometimes less, of your account at a time, you will find that you aren't as emotional about the trades. Even if it goes south, your whole account is not lost. You can still enter into other trades, sometimes at the same time, without having to worry that your whole account will be wiped out with one wrong decision. Considering that even professional traders can have trouble with some of their trades occasionally, this is a good thing to remember.

How will I Manage my Trade?

During this process, we need to consider how we will manage our trades. If you find that a trade will move in your favor, think about how you plan to manage that trade. There are many theories of thought on this idea, and none are necessarily the best ones. Some work best for a few traders, others are preferred in some cases, and so on. You have to determine which one is best for you to help make sure you manage the trades well and get the profits you would like.

For example, many traders, new and professional, like to set up a profit target when they first enter a new trade.

Others will use trail stops to help them because it ensures they will capture some of the larger moves or larger trends that are potentially going to happen. Sometimes you may find yourself in a situation where you want to add to a winning position. This is more a personal preference, so you have to see what works best for you. But it is still critical to see how you would properly manage a winning strategy ahead of time. This ensures you make as much as possible without staying in the market so long you lose out.

The strategy you choose will make a big difference in how you manage your trade. A good strategy will help you know how to enter the market, and when it is time to exit. They can often help us learn how to read many of the charts out there, making it so much easier to pick the right time to get into the trade. If you pick a strategy, use the steps and tips it talks about to manage each trade you use it on. This helps to take the guesswork out and can help you get healthy profits.

While it may seem like these are really simple questions, and we shouldn't even need to ask them, remembering what they are and asking them during each trade will be the trick you need to make sure your options contracts are as successful as possible.

As a beginner, you may ask these questions of others and be surprised at how many never even think about them at all.

Consider the Emotions

As we go through all of this, we must make sure that we can accurately handle all of our emotions along the way. If our emotions start to come into the trade, we instantly lose all of that critical thinking and start making really poor decisions along the way. This is easy to do, which is why a good strategy and some strong stop-loss points can help.

We will talk more about these stop-loss points and strategies later on, but they allow you to make a good plan for your investment right from the beginning. You won't get caught up in emotions because you know exactly when to keep going and when to leave ahead of time. Before entering the trade, you have no skin in the game, so you aren't worried about things going well or things going poorly. You make sound and rational decisions, which will help you along the way. If you wait to make these decisions after you have entered, it is possible the emotions will sneak in and can ruin even the best trade.

Chapter 2: Basics of Trading

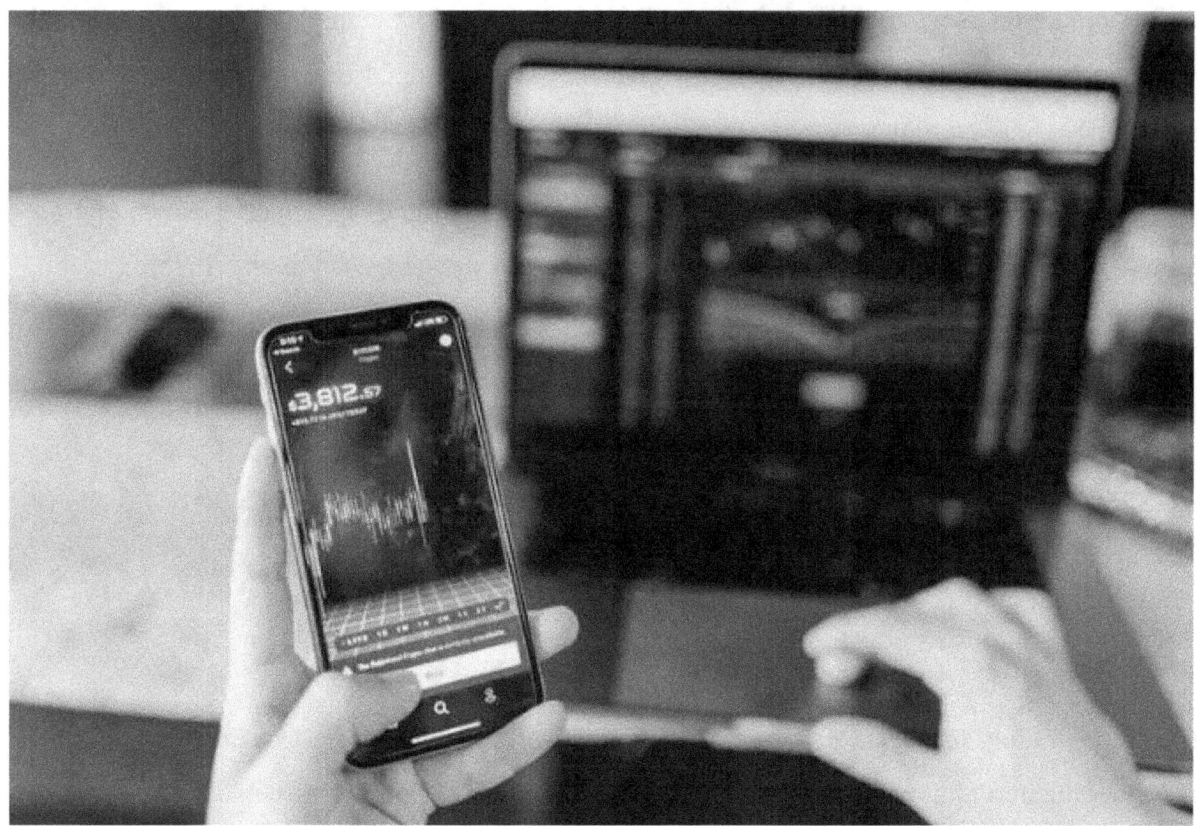

The main method for investing in the forex market, therefore, remains the classic forex market. When you operate on the forex market, you are buying and selling currencies.

However, other financial instruments have been introduced to invest in forex and currencies indices on the forex exchange over the years. We are talking about CFD (contract for difference) and binary options. The main feature of these two financial instruments is the following: when you use them to invest in forex, you will not own the lots you invest in.

That said, for those who do not intend to trade online, it could make little sense. Let's try to clarify. Both CFDs and binary options are contracts between investors and brokers. It's not like the classic forex market, where traders buy and sell among themselves. In CFDs and binary options, the asset movement (in this case the buying and selling of currencies) does not occur.

CFDs and binary options are used to speculate on the performance of the value of equity securities. If the trader's forecast is correct, the operation will lead to a profit; vice versa, if the trader's prediction is wrong, the operation will lead to a loss. So, the mode of operation is similar to the stock market: if I invest on the upside, whether I do it with CFDs or buy currencies, I only earn money if the value increases.

CFDs are also derivative instruments, so they are used to speculate on the performance of asset values. This means that you will never own the asset traded (as opposed to classic forex trading).

Moreover, as with binary options, with CFDs it is possible to trade on:

- Equity securities
- Equity indices
- Forex currencies pairs
- Commodities
- ETF

The online trading strategies are based on mathematical and graphic analysis that can suggest to the trader the best moment to buy and sell. As we have seen today, it is possible to invest in the stock market thanks to online trading, choosing between trading binary options and trading with the forex market.

It is evident right away that there is no suitable trading strategy for all traders, but there are different trading strategies, based on traders and their style of trading. Therefore, it is possible to customize different online trading strategies based on their trading objectives and their intellectual and psychological abilities.

We also recommend using 2 proven techniques not to turn winnings into losses:

Stop loss: it establishes a maximum loss that you are willing to suffer.

Take profit: you place a dynamic exit level that rises slowly.

Stocks vs. Other Investments

In this historical moment, the search for high returns has become almost spasmodic. Unfortunately, central banks' expansionary policy has caused the collapse of yields (now virtually 0). Anyone who wants to get a positive return must take risks.

In this context, many are deciding to invest in stocks. The answer? It certainly is worth it, but it all depends on the modality of the investment.

This is an investment that can still guarantee very high performance, provided, however, you follow some guidelines.

The first tip is to use only affordable platforms to invest in stocks. Among the best, we can remember Plus500 or Markets. These platforms are characterized by the fact that they are very easy to use, even for those who have never worked with the actions but, at the same time, guarantee advanced tools, suitable even for the most experienced traders and their needs. You receive a free bonus at the time of registration that amounts to 7,000 euros for Plus500 and 4,000 euros for Markets. This is additional capital that can operate on the stock markets but cannot be directly withdrawn. If you use the bonus and get profits, these profits can be taken without problems and constraints.

Both Plus500 and Markets are Trading Contracts for Difference (CFD) trading platforms: this is a particularly flexible and easy-to-understand derivative instrument that guarantees the possibility of obtaining high profits both when markets rise, and markets fall. This is the second condition that makes it worthwhile to invest in stocks: if you buy shares directly, you earn only when the markets go up. And in today's financial conditions, it's an immense gamble. It is not convenient to buy shares, the thing that must be done is to subscribe to derivatives (such as CFDs that are very simple) that have underlying actions. Plus500 and Markets are the ideal solutions for investing in stocks and, incidentally, they also allow investing in forex, indices, commodities, bitcoins, etc.

If you want to invest in shares and want to earn money, the advice is to open an account on Markets or Plus500.

The Big Advantage of Stock Investing – Leverage

Through the use of financial leverage (or simply "leverage"), a person can buy or sell financial assets for an amount higher than the capital held and, consequently, to benefit from a higher potential return than that deriving from a direct investment in the underlying and, conversely, to expose yourself to the risk of very significant losses.

Let's see how the concept of leverage works starting from a simple case. Let's assume you have $ 100 available to invest Leverage financial in a stock. Let's assume that the gain or loss expectations are equal to 30%: if things go well, we will have $ 130. Otherwise, we will have $ 70. This is a simple speculation in which we bet on a particular event.

In case we decide to risk more investing and our $ 100, with another $ 900 borrowed, then the investment would take a different articulation because we use a leverage of 10 to 1 (we invest $ 1000 having a capital initial only of 100). If things go well and the stock goes up 30%, we will receive $ 1300; we return the 900 borrowed with a gain of $ 300 on initial capital of 100. So, we get a 300% profit with a stock that gave a 30% return. Obviously, on the $ 900 borrowed we will have to pay interest, but the general principle remains valid: the leverage allows to increase the possible gains.

Considering the case further of the investment in derivatives. Let's assume we buy a derivative that, within a month, gives the right to buy 100 grams of gold at a price set today at $ 5,000. We could physically buy the gold with an outlay of 5000 $ and keep it waiting for the price to rise and then sell it back. If we decide instead to use derivatives, we don't need to have $ 5,000, but only the capital needed to buy the derivative. Let's say that a bank sells for 100 $ the derivative that allows us to buy the same 100 grams of gold in a month at $ 5,000. If in a month the gold is worth 5,500, we can buy it and sell it immediately, realizing a gain of 500 $. With the 100 $ of the derivative price, we make a profit of $ 400, or 400%, at $ 100.

Without using derivatives and leverage, the same $500, I could have earned them only against an investment of $ 5,000, making a profit of 10%.

What are the potentials of its use?

The potential of leveraging is clear. For example, if we decide to invest $ 100 in our possession plus an additional sum of $ 900 borrowed, if the stock depreciated by 30%, we would be left with only $ 700 in hand; having to return the $ 900 borrowed plus interest and considering the $ 100 of our initial investment we would have a loss of over $ 300 on an initial capital of $ 100. Therefore, as a percentage, the loss would be 300% against a reduction in the value of the share of 30%.

Another element to keep in mind is that the different financial levers can be combined: speculation operations are carried out using a "squared lever" with clear reflections on potential potentials.

What may appear to be an interesting tool with positive potential for the investor, on the other hand, presents risks that must be considered. Suppose the financial system as a whole work with a very high leverage and financial institutions lend money to each other to multiply the possible profits.

In that case, the loss of an individual investor can trigger a domino effect by infecting the entire financial market.

Banks are typically entities that operate with a more or less high degree of leverage: against a certain net capital, the total assets in which the resources are invested is generally much higher. For example, a bank with equity of $ 100 and leverage of 20 manages assets for $ 2,000. A loss of 1% of the assets entails the loss of 20% of the equity capital.

The development of the market for the transfer of credit risk (from financial intermediaries to the market) has meant that the traditional bank model, called "originate-and-hold" ("create and hold": the loan remains in the balance sheet until maturity in the bank that provided the loan), has been substituted for many operators from the "originate-to-distribute" ("create and distribute": the intermediary selects the debtors, but then transfers the loan to others, recovering the liquidity and the regulatory capital previously committed or the pure credit risk (credit derivatives), with benefits only on capital requirements), with the effect of a further increase in leverage.

The spread of this second bank model is one factor that explains the crisis triggered on the sub-prime mortgage market.

Property price inflation has supported the issuance of securitized loans and the exponential growth of the related market, allowing banks to make huge profits and, at the same time, increase leverage. But "the money machine" could not last long. In the end, many banks found themselves without sufficient capital to absorb the losses deriving from the inversion of the real estate market trend, resulting in fact as failed companies.

Chapter 3: What is Options Trading?

The first step to consider when engaging in options trading is to have a clear and accurate understanding of an option. Most people barely understand what the stock market is and how it operates, and options are a level above even that. Then we will detail in the rest of the book to learn everything you need to be able to trade options with success. Remember that all forms of investing and trading carry financial risk, and not everyone who invests or trades on the markets will succeed.

What Is an Option?

Options are not restricted to the stock market. The name option gives us a clue as to what these financial instruments are, however. An options contract is one that enables the buyer to have the option to do something. Options contracts can exist in any context where you are interested in buying something. The proverbial example that is used is the option to buy a new home.

Let's say that Jane is moving to her new job in Houston, Texas. She is interested in buying a new home in a good neighborhood that is reasonably close to her job. She has two kids, so she's also interested in buying a home in an area with a low crime rate and good schools.

She finds out that there is a new housing development near her job. She also finds out that it will take about 4 months to have a home ready to move in. Because of the high demand in the area, home prices are changing rapidly. She'd like to lock in a price for a home but wants to look around in the meantime. How can she do that? The answer is she can enter into an options contract with the developer.

The type of homes that Jane is interested in are currently going for $350,000. Jane tells the developer she is willing to buy a house at this price, but she needs 120 days to decide. The developer knows that prices are rapidly increasing, but to make a deal he offers the possibility for Jane to lock in a lot and home for $360,000. She must buy the home on or before the date the contract expires 120 days from the date, she signs it. If she fails to close by that time, the contract expires, and the developer is free to sell the lot to someone else at market prices.

Jane is not taking too much risk because she is not forced to buy the home; she has the option. If prices end up dropping, she can simply let the option contract expire. If prices stay about the same or keep rising, and she doesn't find another home she is interested in, Jane can go ahead and exercise her rights under the contract and buy the house for $360,000. This is true even if the price of new homes in the area has jumped to $400,000 when the contract expires. So, by locking in a price, Jane may have put herself in a position where she could save a significant amount of money yet get the home (investment) that she wanted.

While laws may vary based upon the given specific contract type, generally speaking, the contracts themselves can be bought and sold. The contract itself becomes valuable because of the *underlying* asset (in this case, the home), and the ability to buy that asset at a fixed price. In an environment of rising prices, this can provide a big advantage to buyers. In many cases, the buyers won't go through with the contract. Executing the contract is called *exercising* the contract. Of course, if home prices in the area were to rise to $400,000, it would be worth exercising this option's contract.

Jane may not want to do so. Maybe she found a different home more to her liking. However, since the contract has obvious value, she could sell it to someone else. Ever since financial instruments were invented, secondary markets were created soon afterward, where people traded them. Options are no exception.

Since an option derives its value from an underlying asset that is not directly traded or even owned by the person who buys the option, it is called a *derivative*. The media often talks about derivatives as extremely exotic and complex, but it is nothing more than that. A derivative is a financial instrument or contract that derives its value from an underlying asset.

Options on Stocks

The basic concepts of options that we described above apply to options on stocks. Since we now understand those basic concepts, let's define the specifics of options contracts on stocks. It turns out that options contracts on stocks are slightly more complicated than what we've described so far, but it's not complicated if you take it step-by-step.

The first thing to note is underlying. As far as options on stocks are concerned, its corresponding asset is 10 shares of a specific stock. That stock is a stock of a publicly-traded company on a major stock exchange. Options on stocks also include index funds. So, you can trade options on Apple, Facebook, or Boeing. You can also trade options on SPY, DIA, and QQQ, which are exchange-traded funds for the most significant stock markets such as the Dow Jones Industrial Average, the Standard & Poors 500, and NASDAQ 100, respectively.

For example, using a home purchase, we only talked about the option for someone to buy the home – we never considered having the option to sell a home. But with stocks, both concepts are equally important. The most basic concept is imagining having an option that would give you the possibility of purchasing those 10 shares of a given stock at a pre-determined sale point on or before the contract's expiration date. This kind of deal is known as a *call option*.

You can see that in a market of rising prices, a call option favors the buyer. The potential buyer can lock in a price. If they choose to do so, if the price per share rises by a significant amount (and by significant we mean significant enough to earn a profit if you turned around and sold the shares on the market), the buyer can buy shares at a discount.

In an environment of rising prices, since the option contract would give buyers such an advantage, the contract itself becomes more valuable. With everything else remaining equal, the price of the said contract will be going up in a market of rising prices. People will be bidding up the price as more investors excitedly want to get their hands on the option.

There are going to be two types of buyers in the marketplace. Some buyers are interested in getting a hold of the stock at a discount price. Others are simply hoping or anticipating that prices will continue rising, so they anticipate that the price of the option will be higher in the future. In other words, they want to buy the option, and then turn around and sell it for a higher price a few days or weeks later at a higher price to make a profit *from the option contract itself.*

When we are talking about anticipating making a profit from future price changes, this is called speculating. The term speculating is associated with *trading*, which can be defined as short term purchase and sale of a financial asset with the sole intent of generating profits. It is important to keep this concept distinct from *investing*. The first difference between trading and investing in the time frame. Trading is generally done on short-term time frames of one year or less. In contrast, investing generally means five years or more. Investing is a long-term commitment to something you believe in.

Of course, investors hope that their assets are going to increase in value as well. Otherwise, they wouldn't invest. But they are in it for the long haul and will not be getting rid of their assets soon after they acquire them. The reasons for investing often go beyond simple profit. Investors may be passionate about the companies they invest in and the products they offer or believe that the companies they invest in represent the economy's future. They may also take a broad view, and invest in index funds, based on the idea that the economy will grow with time.

It is crucial to have a clear understanding of the difference between trading and investing, and understanding what "speculating" is, as an options trader. As we'll see later, you might have to express that you understand the difference as an options trader to satisfy regulators.

Put Options

Now let's turn our attention to the other major type of option on the equities market. The option we are going to be discussing is known as a "put option." This kind of contract entitles the buyer to acquire a set quantity of stock at a pre-determined sale point. That might appear to you as somewhat bizarre at first, so why would anyone want to do that? The answer is that put options are valuable to buyers in a market of declining prices. If the stock is dropping significantly below the fixed price agreed upon in the options contract, it makes sense to either do one. If you already own the shares, maybe you purchased them at a much higher price, and you want to limit your losses. In that case, a put option allows you to cut your losses at a given price point that may be significantly above the market valuation. You don't have to worry if the market price keeps dropping, you can sell your shares at a price agreed to in the contract at any time before it expires. So, in this case, a put option can be a form of insurance for a buyer who has invested in many shares.

It's also possible for speculators to profit. The first case is where you want to sell the stock. To do this, you wait until the stock price drops low enough to make a move on the option that would be profitable. So, you buy the 100 shares and then sell them to exercise your rights under the option. Of course, the way this would work is to sell them to the originator of the options contract, who is obligated to honor the contract and buy the shares.

Chapter 4: Why Trade Options?

This is a common question people are asking. Why do you want to exchange options?

Well, the first reason for this is to protect and control your risk. If you take a big risk, trading options is the way to protect yourself so that you don't lose all your money. It gives you full control of how and where your money is going.

But one thing you should know is that trading options should not be done with your eyes closed. You're going to have to keep an eye on the market. And if you don't, it's going to shoot you back.

Let's get started now.

Hedge and Speculation

Hedging and Speculation are the first two things you should learn before you spend a single penny on trading options. This is what's going to get you going and how you're expected to handle trading options.

Hedging is when you fear something could go wrong. It doesn't mean that anything is going to go wrong, it's just a way to protect yourself (I mean your money) if things start to go wrong.

Hedging is the way to ensure your investment if rates start to fall. In other words, hiding is your defense against losing a lot of money. Hedging is used by large companies and institutional investors to cover themselves.

On the other hand, if you have no knowledge of the underlying asset (stock, bond, or commodity) when using options as a hedging strategy, then according to experts, you will certainly lose money. This is because you're trying to hedge too much to buy premiums on something you don't know about. This means that instead of taking a gamble and growing your income, you're going to lose your insurance money.

However, if done properly, hedging is a perfect way to shield yourself from failure.

Next is speculation. But this is very dangerous.

There are three ways that any investor makes a profit – when the price goes up, when the price goes down, and when the price moves sideways (meaning, the price stays or goes up and down within the range).

A lot of money can be made from speculation. Speculation may be rendered by researching and analyzing the market. This includes assessing and forecasting patterns and finding out where the market is heading from the present point of view. This can be a big advantage if you're familiar with the market and have good knowledge of the underlying asset.

But as I said before, speculation is very risky. An investor who wants to make a profit as a speculator must be able to correctly predict the trajectory of the asset price (whether it will rise or fall), the timing of that direction, and the magnitude (the price will change by how much).

Advantages and Drawbacks in Trading Options

We do accept that selling options are difficult. But once you grasp it, it's going to be an ability that you know like the back of your hand. The best part of options trading is that you can make a profit from the price change of the underlying asset without directly investing in the asset.

And as I mentioned earlier, investing in options is actually cheaper than investing in the actual asset. Plus, if you invest directly in the asset, you will have less leverage. In short, by selling options, you now have access to more money than you would have initially had.

And if you add it up, leverage, capital, and so on, you can find that an investor will potentially make more money per actual dollar invested compared to investing directly in the asset. Often with options, an investor can only lose a fixed sum of money, which is effectively the premium he/she has paid.

This means that if you don't place anything in the premium, you're not going to lose everything. This is the safest thing to do if you're just trying to test the water, and you're not ready to go all in.

Another great benefit of Options Trading is that you can use hedging as an insurance strategy to shield yourself from losses that are getting too large. This ensures that you can also shield yourself from extreme swings in the stock market. I would strongly recommend that you begin with as much hedging as possible to reduce your losses.

Another advantage is that you can make money even if the stock doesn't make money. It's because of the ability to trade up, down, or sideways to maximize your power and income. You'll see the stock price dropping several times, and you can still make a profit at the end of it.

Plus, commissions are much less active in trading options (now you know why stockbrokers are advising you about it). And if you want to go through an online broker, those commissions are even smaller because they want to beat their competition.

Besides, trading options are flexible. It helps you to respond based on where the price is going. It gives you the freedom to participate in more than one business as well. This means you can invest in everything from agriculture to foreign currency. Plus, you don't have to spend a lot of money like large companies. All you need is a minimum sum, and you can start making money.

Last but not least, and this one is a biggie, the pace of having your profit in hand. Yeah, as soon as the stock increases, you'll get your benefit so that you can start investing in other markets or stocks. The pace of the market helps you to invest in more markets at the same time and make more money out of it. And unlike other forms of day trading, options trading is just a short-term bet. This means that even if you make an inaccurate prediction, you'll lose money within a few months instead of waiting for years to lose money because of that error.

Taxes are a detriment when it comes to trading options. Yeah, you're going to have to pay taxes on everything you do, except in those exceptional situations. So, make sure you fill out your IRA form to make sure you keep tax tabs before you start investing.

Moreover, unlike shares, there is no certificate of deposit when it comes to options. It's all paying rights, so it doesn't give you evidence of possession. This means that you will not be able to justify to people the ownership of the stock unless it is a stock certificate.

And then there's a matter of ambiguity. It's a little frightening when you're investing in something you don't know about. That's why most investors make sure they have an in-depth, detailed knowledge of what they're investing in because it can quickly turn into a gamble that isn't worth the winnings.

It's important to know your plan. And be sure to start small and slow to prevent losing high.

It's almost like driving a car. It's all scary when you're driving for the first time. But as you spend more and more time behind the wheel, you know the tricks of the trade, and you instantly become the best driver.

Chapter 5: Options Contracts – The Basics (Part I)

In our introductory discussion, we will be focusing on the most basic way to get involved in options, which involves buying options contracts based on bets you make on whether future stock prices will rise or fall. Later we will see that you can also write or sell options contracts and that the contracts themselves are traded on the markets.

What is an Options Contract?

An options contract sounds fancy but it's a pretty simple concept.

- It's a contract. That means it's a legal agreement between a buyer and a seller.
- It allows the purchaser of the contract to purchase or dispose of an asset with a fixed amount.
- The purchase is optional – so the buyer of the contract does not have to buy or sell the asset.
- The contract has an expiration date, so the purchaser – if they choose to exercise their right – must make the trade on or before the expiration date.
- The purchaser of the contract pays a non-refundable fee for the contract.

While the focus of this book is on options contracts related to the stock market, some options contracts take place in all aspects of daily life including real estate and speculation. A simple example illustrates the concept of an options contract.

Suppose you are itching to buy a BMW and you've decided the model you want must be silver. You drop by a local dealer and it turns out they don't have a silver model in stock. The dealer claims he can get you one by the end of the month. You say you'll take the car if the dealer can get it by the last day of the month and he'll sell it to you for $67,500. He agrees and requires you to put a $3,000 deposit on the car.

If the last day of the month arrives and the dealer hasn't produced the car, then you're freed from the contract and get your money back. In the event he does produce the car at any date before the end of the month, you have the option to buy it or not. If you really wanted the car you can buy it, but of course, you can't be forced to buy the car, and maybe you've changed your mind in the interim.

The right is there but not the obligation to purchase, in short, no pressure if you decided not to push through with the purchase of the car. If you decide to let the opportunity pass, however, since the dealer met his end of the bargain and produced the car, you lose the $3,000 deposit.

In this case, the dealer, who plays the role of the writer of the contract, must follow through with the sale based upon the agreed-upon price.

Suppose that when the car arrives at the dealership, BMW announces it will no longer make silver cars. As a result, prices of new silver BMWs that were the last ones to roll off the assembly line, skyrocket. Other dealers are selling their silver BMWs for $100,000. However, since this dealer entered into an options contract with you, he must sell the car to you for the pre-agreed price of $67,500. You decide to get the car and drive away smiling, knowing that you saved $32,500 and that you could sell it at a profit if you wanted to.

The situation here is capturing the essence of options contracts, even if you've never thought of haggling with a car dealer in those terms.

An option is in a sense a kind of bet. In the example of the car, the bet is that the dealer can produce the exact car you want within the specified period and at the agreed-upon price. The dealer is betting too. He bets that the pre-agreed price is a good one for him. Of course, if BMW stops making silver cars, then he's made the wrong bet.

It can work the other way too. Let's say that instead of BMW deciding not to make silver cars anymore when your car is being driven onto the lot, another car crashes into it. Now your silver BMW has a small dent on the rear bumper with some scratches. As a result, the car has immediately declined in value. But if you want the car, since you've agreed to the options contract, you must pay $67,500, even though with the dent it's only really worth $55,000. You can walk away and lose your $3,000 or pay what is now a premium price on a damaged car.

Another example that is commonly used to explain options contracts is the purchase of a home to be built by a developer under the agreement that certain conditions are met. The buyer will be required to put a non-refundable down payment or deposit on the home. Let's say that the developer agrees to build them the home for $300,000 provided that a new school is built within 5 miles of the development within one year. So, the contract expires within a year. At any time during the year, the buyer has the option to go forward with the construction of the home for $300,000 if the school is built. The developer has agreed to the price no matter what. So if the housing market in general and the construction of the school, in particular, drive up demand for housing in the area, and the developer is selling new homes that are now priced at $500,000, he has to sell this home for $300,000 because that was the price agreed to when the contract was signed. The home buyer got what they wanted, being within 5 miles of the new school with the home price fixed at $300,000. The developer was assured of the sale but missed out on the unknown, which was the skyrocketing price that occurred as a result of increased demand. On the other hand, if the school isn't built and the buyers don't exercise their option to buy the house before the contract expires at one year, the developer can pocket the $20,000 cash.

What is an Options Contract on the Stock Market?

An options contract on the stock market is somewhat analogous to the fictitious situation we just described w/ the car. In the case of the car, we saw that unforeseen events can make the bet made by the buyer and the car dealer profitable or not. The same thing happens in the stock market. Of course, in the case of the car, the buyer is simply hoping to get the car they want at what they perceive to be a bargain price, although if BMW really stopped making silver cars, they might sell it to a third party and then get a white one from the dealer. However, in most cases, the buyer wants the car. That isn't the case when it comes to options with stocks.

On the stock market, we are betting on the future price itself, and the shares of stock will be bought or sold at a profit if things work out. The key point is the buyer of the options contract is not hoping to acquire the shares and hold them for a long period like a traditional investor. Instead, you're hoping to make a bet on the price of the stock, secure that price, and then be able to trade the shares on that price no matter what happens on the actual markets. We will illustrate this with an example.

Call Options

A call is a type of options contract that provides the option to purchase an asset at the agreed-upon amount at the designated time or deadline. The reason you would do this is if you felt that the price of a given stock would increase in price over the specified period. Let's illustrate with an example.

Suppose that Acme Communications makes cutting edge smartphones. The rumors are that they will announce a new smartphone in the next three weeks that is going to take the market by storm, with customers lined out the door to make preorders.

The current price that Acme Communications is trading at is $44.25 a share. The current pricing of an asset is termed as the *spot price*. Put another way, the spot price is the actual amount that you would be paying for the shares as you would buy them from the stock market right now.

Nobody really knows if the stock price will go up when the announcement is made, or if the announcement will even be made. But you've done your research and are reasonably confident these events will take place. You also have to estimate how much the shares will go up and based on your research you think it's going to shoot up to $65 a share by the end of the month.

You enter into an options contract for 100 shares at $1 per share. You pay this fee to the brokerage that is writing the options contract. In total, for 100 shares you pay $100.

The price that is paid for an options contract is $100. This price is called the *premium*.

You don't get the premium back. It's a fee that you pay no matter what. If you make a profit, then it's all good. But if your bet is wrong, then you'll lose the premium. For the buyer of an options contract, the premium is their risk.

You'll want to set a price that you think is going to be lower than the level to which the price per share will rise. The price that you agree to is called the *strike price*. For this contract, you set your strike price at $50.

Remember, exercising your right to buy the shares is optional. You'll only buy the shares if the price goes high enough that you'll make a profit on the trade. If the shares never go above $50, say they reach $48, you are not obligated to buy them. And why would you? As part of the contract deal, you'd be required to buy them at $50.

We'll say that the contract is entered on the 1st of August, and the deadline is the third Friday in August. If the price goes higher than your strike price during that time, you can exercise your option.

Let's say that as the deadline approaches, things go basically as you planned. Acme Communications announces its new phone, and the stock starts climbing. The stock price on the actual market (the spot price) goes up to $60.

Now the seller is required to sell you the shares at $50 a share. You buy the shares, and then you can immediately dispose of these at a quality or optimal amount, or $60 a share. You make a profit of $10 a share, not taking into account any commissions or fees.

The Call Seller

The call seller who enters into the options contract with the buyer is obligated to sell the shares to the buyer of the options contract at the strike price. If the contract sets the strike price at $50 a share for 100 shares, the seller must sell the stock at that price even if the market price goes up to any higher price, such as $70 a share. The call seller keeps the premium. So, if the buyer doesn't exercise their option, the call seller still gets the money from the premium.

Derivative Contracts

You probably heard about derivatives or derivative contracts during the 2008 financial crisis. While they can be designed in complex ways, the concept of a derivative contract is pretty simple. What this means is that the contract is based on some underlying asset. For an options contract, the asset is the stock that you agree to buy or sell. The contracts themselves can and are bought and sold. That is why you may have heard about people trading in derivatives. The stock that is the subject of an options contract is called the underlying.

So, if you buy an options contract using the Apple stock price as a basis, the term "underlying" would apply to the stock from Apple.

Profits from the Call

Keep in mind the brokerage may have some additional fees. However, using our numbers remember that we paid a premium of $1 per share, and the strike price was $50. Computing for profit is one of the basics when it comes to trading. It is where profits are determined and forecasted for future options to buy or sell.

The profit per share was:

Profit = $60 − ($50 + $1) = $9 per share

The contract was for 100 shares, so the total profit would be $90.

What Happens if the Strike Price isn't Reached?

The strike price is the fundamental piece of information you need to keep in mind when trading options. If the strike price isn't reached, then the option will simply expire and be worthless. The difference between the current market price or spot price and the strike price is a measure of the profit per share that you will make.

For example, $100 is the price of the stock, and the strike price is $75, then the profit (disregarding fees) will be $25. If the strike price was $95, then the profit per share would only be $5. While the payoff from a strike price that is closer to the actual market price is smaller, it's more likely to pay off than a strike price that predicts a big move.

Why Purchase a Call Option

The reason that you purchase an options contract is to reduce your risk. When you buy an options contract, the only money you're putting at risk is the premium. In the case of our hypothetical example, that is $100. If the stock doesn't surpass the strike price, you can simply walk away from the deal and only lose the $100.

You could, of course, buy the stocks outright and hope to profit. To buy 100 shares, you'll have to invest substantially more money:

100 x $44.25 = $4,425.

If the stock goes up value, then you'll make some money. However, suppose that your hunch about the markets was wrong. Maybe Acme Communications, rather than announcing a new phone that will be in high demand, instead reveals that their next phone will be delayed for a year.

If you decide to unload the stocks you bought for $4,425, you will only get $4,000, and you'll have lost $425.

On the other hand, you can see how you reduced your risk by purchasing a call option. In that case, you won't exercise your right to buy the stock and only lose the premium. Your total loss would be $100.

The Flexibility of Options

In normal stock trading, you're betting in one direction, that the value of the stock will go up with time. And you're battling the opposite, hoping to avoid losses if the stock declines.

Options open the door to making a profit when stocks decline in value. Of course, it depends on being able to make the right call, but if you bet on a stock losing value and you're right, you can make substantial profits. Timing and the size of your trade will be important too, and you'll have to stay focused on the strike price and the current market price of the underlying.

Put Options

A call option is the choice to buy a stock if it reaches the strike price. Now let's look at the opposite situation. A put is an option contract where you get the right but not the obligation to sell a stock before the contract expires. You bet that it's going to decrease to at least $35 a share, so you buy a put option with a strike price of $35 a share. If your bet that the stock will decline in value and you're correct, let's say it drops to $30 a share, then you can make a $5 per share profit on the sale. If the stock meets the strike price, the seller of the put is obligated to purchase the stock at that price. In other words, even though the stock has dropped in value to $30 a share on the market, they must buy the shares from you at $35 a share.

Let's suppose that instead it only drops to $38 a share. In this case, you don't have to sell and simply walk away from the deal having paid the premium. So once again, as was the case with a call option, the premium is really the only money that you risk as to the buyer.

The seller of a put option must buy the stock from you at the strike price if you exercise your option. If the strike price is $35 but for some reason, the stock crashes to $1, the seller of the put must buy the shares from you at $35.

Why Buy a Put Option?

The answer is simple – when you buy stocks the usual way, you don't make any money from the declining values of stocks. You lose money. With a put option, it gives you the possibility of betting on the stock losing value.

Summary: Buyers of Options

The buyer of an options contract:

- Must pay the premium. This is non-refundable, so the premium is the minimum amount of capital you invest and is the amount you risk.
- You are not obligated to buy or sell any stock even when the deadline arrives.
- You have purchased the right to buy or sell the stock.
- If you buy a call, then you have the option to purchase the expiry of the agreement. If you buy a put, you have the option to sell the stock when the expiry arrives. The option to sell only falls in instances when there is a marked difference between the market price and your own strike price; with the market price being too low.

Summary: Sellers of Calls and Puts

Later we'll see that you may want to sell options and there are good reasons for doing so. Right now, we'll just summarize the general principles.

- The seller of an options contract will keep the premium no matter what. So, if the buyer doesn't exercise their option, you keep the premium as profit.
- If the buyer of a call option exercises their option to buy the stock, you must sell it to them at the strike price. So, if the strike price is $40 but the current market price is $65,

you are missing out on a large profit per share. However, as we'll see later this can still be profitable.

- If the buyer exercises their right on a put contract, you must buy the stock from them at the deadline.

Number of Shares

The number of shares in one options contract is 100 shares. Typically, traders will trade multiple contracts. To you'll get the profit per share and then calculate total profit as (profit per share * 100 shares * # of contracts).

Now let's get familiar with the industry jargon so you can have a better understanding of what is going on when you start trading.

Chapter 6: Variety of Options and Related Styles

Call Options

These options provide you with the right to buy stock labeled as an underlying one. With Call Options, you can buy not only stocks but also commodities, bonds, or any other instrument that has a specified price, otherwise known as the strike price, within a specific timeframe. Call Options contract gives you the right to buy, but you don't have an obligation to do so. A person who is bullish on the stock is usually the investor who expects the value of the stock to increase shortly. This kind of investor buys call options and manages them in the specified time frame. Again, let's take an example.

Let's say that the investor we will name Mr. B thinks that next month CCC Company will have more significant earnings for the stock, and the stock will have a higher value. In this case, Mr. B buys a call option for the CCC Company's stock for 20 dollars, for example. The contract of the option has a term that Mr. B can buy up to 100 shares from CCC Company within the next two months. The strike price for these shares within this time frame is 100 dollars. So, if the value of the stock goes 100 dollars in the next period, Mr. B won't exercise his option, which means that he will lose his first 20 dollars of investment (remember, if the option is not exercised within the specific time frame, or two months in this particular case, the contract expires and becomes worthless).

On the other hand, if the value of the stock goes over 100 dollars, and the next price is 130 dollars, for example, Mr. B can exercise his option. He can now buy the stock for 100 dollars and sell it for 130 dollars on the market. The risk that Mr. B took paid off, and he earned a significant profit.

Put Options

These options have opposite traits from the Call Options. Put Options represent the contract in which the purchaser has the right to sell his or her stocks. These stocks, like all others, must be sold for the strike price (a price that's been specified for a specific time). Put Options, like Call

Options, give the right to sell, but they are not obligatory. Now we can return to Mr. B and observe him as an investor who is bearish on a particular stock.

In this example, Mr. B thinks that the price of the stock he is interested in will decrease, and, in that case, he will purchase a put option. According to Mr. B, the stock that CCC Company has is overpriced, and its value will go lower in the next two months. Let's say that Mr. B buys a Put Option on this stock for 20 dollars again. Contract of the Put Option gives Mr. B a chance to sell the stock he bought from CCC Company for 120 dollars in the next 60 days. So if the stock value increases more than 120 dollars per share, Mr. B won't have to exercise his Put Option, the time frame will pass, and the option will become worthless, which means that he would lose only his initial capital of 20 dollars. However, if the value of the stock goes down and the price goes from 120 dollars to 90 dollars, for example, the Put Option will be exercised, and Mr. B can sell this stock for 120 dollars per share. Once again, he judged correctly, and he has made a considerable profit.

How to Make a Profit Using Call Options and Put Options

There are many ways for a trader to use Call Options and Put Options and be successful in the process. The best way to show some of the most efficient ways to use these options is by using real numbers. Imagine you want to buy shares from US Bank. Let's suppose that the bank currently sells them for the price of 200 dollars per share and that you conclude that this number is going to go up since the shares are underpriced. Let's also suppose that the predicted amount of time that the shares will need to increase their value is a few months from now. At the moment, you don't have enough capital to buy 100 shares from the US Bank. However, you still want to make some profit from the stock that will rise in value according to your estimation. If this is the case, you can use Call Option and buy it for the stock. This way, you reduce the cost, and you pay only a fraction of the original stock price. Once that you purchased the Call Option, you gained the right to buy 100 shares of US Bank stock for 200 dollars per share in the next two months. One of your doubts might immediately be how you are supposed to buy that stock for 200 dollars per share in the next 60 days when you don't have the initial amount of money for that in the first place? Well, the thing is that you are not under obligation actually to buy the stock if you want to make money. If your estimation is correct, and in the next period, the value of the stock goes over 200 dollars per share, the Call Option that you bought would increase in value too. In other words, your option contract value rises with the value of the stock price. Keeping this in mind, you get the opportunity to sell your Call Options contract to make money, not the shares. That is the real connection because once when the stock price rises, your contract is worth a lot more than the money you invested in buying it.

A similar thing happens if you purchase the Put Options contract. The only difference is that your estimation has to be decreased in the stock value rather than prices going higher. Once when the underlying security price goes down, the price of your Put Option will go up. The more that the stock price falls, the more expensive your contract becomes. Using options in both cases means that you can make a profit regardless of the rise or fall of the stock prices.

Option Styles

There are various styles of options used in the trader's market, and it is essential to understand them. However, most of the options that are used in everyday trading belong to one of the main styles—American style or European style. These two categories are often called vanilla options, and their main difference is the time of execration for both types of options.

American Options

The first style of options that we will introduce is also one of the two that are used most often. These options are called American Options, and their main characteristic is that they can be exercised at any point as long as the option hasn't reached its expiration date. American Options are also considered to be the most frequent type of contract traded on the market when it comes to future exchanges.

European Options

On the other hand, have a different excretion policy. The expiration date of the option has to be defined in the contract, which means that the option can be exercised only during that specific period. The type of market called 'over the counter' or OTC for short is the market in which European Options are traded the most.

However, the value of American and European Options is calculated differently. Additionally, the expiration date is also different for each of these styles. For American Options, the expiration date is pre-determined before the investor purchases the contract. The American Option always expires on the third Saturday of the following month. Contrarily, the European Option becomes worthless on Friday—a day before the third Saturday of the specified month. There are a few similarities between these so-called vanilla options too. They both have the rule of buying and selling at the strike price, and they both include pay-off. Furthermore, whether you calculate pay off for the Call or Put Options, the process is the same, and it usually means that the strike price for these options is the same most of the time.

Exotic Options

As we already mentioned, vanilla options are the two main styles that investors use while trading. However, many other option styles should be aware of. These other styles that are not that frequent are called Exotic Options.

Bermuda Options

In this case, are a style of option that qualifies as something in between American and European versions? The critical difference is that Bermuda Options can be exercised on more than a few dates as long as the contract is valid.

Barrier Options

On the other hand, there are Barrier Options. These options are the most different ones so far, and the reason is that there is a border that needs to be passed to get the payoff for the underlying security price. This is the case for both Call and Put Options. Barrier Options are divided into four categories:

- "Down and Out" Barrier Options – the purchaser of this option has the right (but like in every other case, no obligation) to buy or sell shares, depending on the type of option that he chooses. The condition is that whether these underlying assets are bought or sold, it has to be done using an already determined strike price. The strike price, however, mustn't go lower than a barrier that is pre-determined with the option contract until the expiration date. If by any chance, the price of the owner's shares goes below this barrier, the option loses every value, and that is why it was named "down and out."

- "Down and In" Barrier Options – this option is the total opposite of the "down and out" category. An investor who has this option should know that the only time when the "down and in barrier" has value is when the price of all assets that are underlying and allowed to be purchased by the contract goes below the barrier that was pre-determined for that particular option until it expires. The purchaser has the right to sell or buy shares (again, depending on the type of purchased option) if the barrier was crossed. This trade also has to be done before the expiration date is due and at the strike price.

- "Up and Out" Barrier Options – this category of Barrier Options is similar to "down and out." The main distinction is the fact that the barrier itself is placed differently. In this case, "up and out" means that if the price of any underlying asset being purchased increases above the barrier predetermined by the contract, the option will lose its value.

- "Up and In" Barrier Options – unlike "up and out," this category has similarities with "down and in" options rather than "down and out." The barrier, in this case, is set above the current value of any underlying asset purchased by the investor. The only time that this kind of option carries value is when the price of the stock reaches the placed barrier before the contract expires.

Chapter 7: Covered Calls

Covered Calls

This strategy is called covered calls. By covered, we mean that you've got an asset that you own that covers the potential sale of the underlying stocks. In other words, you already own the shares of stocks. Now, why would you want to write a call option on stocks you already own? The basis of this strategy is that you don't expect the stock price to move very much during the lifetime of the options contract, but you want to generate money over the short term in the form of premiums that you can collect. This can help you generate a short-term income stream; you must structure your calls carefully.

Setting up covered calls is relatively low risk and will help you get familiar with many of the aspects of options trading. While it's probably not going to make you rich overnight, it's a good way to learn the tools of the trade.

Covered Calls Involve a Long Position

To create a covered call, you need to own at least 100 shares of stock in one underlying equity. When you create a call, you're going to be offering potential buyers a chance to buy these shares from you. Of course, the strategy is that you're only going to sell high, but your real goal is to get the income stream from the premium.

The premium is a one-time non-refundable fee. If a buyer purchases your call option and pays you the premium, that money is yours. No matter what happens after that, you've got that cash to keep. If the stock doesn't reach the strike price, the contract will expire, and you can create a new call option on the same underlying shares. Of course, if the stock price does pass the strike price, the buyer of the contract will probably exercise their right to buy the shares. You will still earn money on the trade, but the risk is you're giving up the potential to earn as much money that could have been earned on the trade.

You write a covered call option that has a strike price of $67. Suppose that for some unforeseen reason the shares skyrocket to $90 a share. The buyer of your call option will be able to purchase the shares from you at $67. So, you've gained $2 a share. However, you've missed out on the chance to sell the shares at a profit of $35 a share. Instead, the investor who purchased the call option from you will turn around and sell the shares on the markets for the actual spot price and they will reap the benefits.

However, you really haven't lost anything. You have earned the premium plus sold your shares of stock for a modest profit.

That risk – that the stocks will rise to a price that is much higher than the strike price - always exists, but if you do your homework, you're going to be offering stocks that you don't expect to change much in price over the lifetime of your call. So, suppose instead that the price only rose to $68. The price exceeded the strike price so the buyer may exercise their option. In that case, you are still missing out on some profit that you could have had otherwise, but it's a small amount and we're not taking into account the premium.

If the stock price doesn't exceed the strike price over the length of the contract, then you get to keep the premium and you get to keep the shares. The premium is yours to keep no matter what.

In reality, in most situations, a covered call is going to be a win-win situation for you.

Covered Calls Are a Neutral Strategy

A covered call is known as a "neutral" strategy. Investors create covered calls for stocks in their portfolio where they only expect small moves over the lifetime of the contract. Moreover, investors will use covered calls on stocks that they expect to hold for the long term. It's a way to earn money on the stocks during a period in which the investor expects that the stock won't move much at price and so have no earning potential from selling.

An Example of a Covered Call

Let's say that you own 100 shares of Acme Communications. It's currently trading at $40 a share. Over the next several months, nobody is expecting the stock to move very much, but as an investor, you feel Acme Communications has solid long-term growth potential. To make a little bit of money, you sell a call option on Acme Communications with a strike price of $43. Suppose that the premium is $0.78 and that the call option lasts 3 months.

For 100 shares, you'll earn a total premium payment of $0.78 x 100 = $78. No matter what happens, you pocket the $78.

Now let's say that over the next three months the stock drops a bit in price so that it never comes close to the strike price, and at the end of the three months, it's trading at $39 a share.

The options contract will expire, and it's worthless. The buyer of the options contract ends up empty-handed. You have a win-win situation. You've earned the extra $78 per 100 shares, and you still own your shares at the end of the contract.

Now let's say that the stock does increase a bit in value. Over time, it jumps up to $42, and then to $42.75, but then drops down to $41.80 by the time the options contract expires. In this scenario, you're finding yourself in a much better position. In this case, the strike price of $43 was never reached, so the buyer of the call option is again left out in the cold. You, on the other hand, keep the premium of $78, and you still get to keep the shares of stock. This time since the shares have increased in value, you're a lot better off than you were before, so it's really a win-win situation for YOU, even though it's a losing situation for the poor soul who purchased your call.

Sadly, there is another possibility, that the stock price exceeds the strike price before the contract expires. In that case, you're required to sell the stock. You still end up in a position that isn't all that bad, however. You didn't lose any actual money, but you lost a potential profit. You still get the premium of $78, plus the earnings from the sale of the 100 shares at the strike price of $43.

A covered call is almost a zero-risk situation because you never actually lose money even though if the stock price soars, you obviously missed out on an opportunity. You can minimize that risk by choosing stocks you use for a covered call option carefully. For example, if you hold shares in a pharmaceutical company that is rumored to be announcing a cure for cancer in two months, you probably don't want to use those shares for a covered call. A company that has more long-term prospects but probably isn't going anywhere in the next few months is a better bet.

How to Go about Creating a Covered Call

To create a covered call, you'll need to own 100 shares of stock. While you don't want to risk a stock that is likely to take off shortly, you don't want to pick a total dud either. There is always someone willing to buy something – at the right price. But you want to go with a decent stock so that you can earn a decent premium.

You start by getting online at your brokerage and looking up the stock online. When you look up stocks online, you'll be able to look at their "option chain" which will give you information from a table on premiums that are available for calls on this stock. You can see these listed under the bid price. The bid price is given on a per-share basis, but a call contract has 100 shares. If your bid price is $1.75, then the actual premium you're going to get is $1.75 x 100 = $175.

An important note is that the further out the expiration date, the higher the premium. A good rule of thumb is to pick an expiry that is between two and three months from the present date. Remember that the longer you go, the higher the risk because that increases the odds that the stock price will exceed the strike price and you'll end up having to sell the shares.

You have an option (no pun intended) with the premium you want to charge. Theoretically, you can set any price you want. Of course, that requires a buyer willing to pay that price for you to actually make the money. A more reasonable strategy is to look at prices people are currently requesting for call options on this stock. You can do this by checking the asking price for the call options on the stock. You can also see prices that buyers are currently offering by looking at the bid prices. For an instant sale, you can simply set your price to a bid price that is already out there. If you want to go a little bit higher, you can submit the order and then wait until someone comes along to buy your call option at the bid price.

To sell a covered call, you select "sell to open."

Benefits of Covered Calls

- A covered call is a relatively low-risk option. The worst-case scenario is that you'll be out of your shares but earn a small profit, a smaller profit than you could have made if you had not created the call contract and simply sold your shares. However, you also get the premium.

- A covered call allows you to generate income from your portfolio in the form of premiums.
- If you don't expect any price moves on the stock in the near term and you plan on holding it long term, it's a reasonable strategy to generate income without taking much risk.

Risks of Covered Calls

- Covered calls can be a risk if you're bullish on the stock, and your expectations are realized, and there is a price spike. In that case, you've traded the small amount of income of the premium with a voluntary cap of the strike price for the potential upside you could have had if you had simply held the stock and sold it at the high price.

If the stock price plummets, while you still get the premium, the stocks will be worthless unless they rebound over the long term. You shouldn't use a call option on stocks that you expect to be on the path to a major drop in the coming months. In that case, rather than writing a covered call, you should simply sell the stocks and take your losses. Alternatively, you can continue holding the stocks to see if they rebound over the long term.

Chapter 8: How Prices Are Determined

Pricing is a complex subject when it comes to options trading. Not only is the price of an option based on the value of the asset, but other external factors have influence.

As an options trader, you want to make sure that you maximize your efforts to make a profit. Learning how to determine the prices you should pay for options is one of the basic ways that you can ensure that your yield is as high as it can be. You do not want to be stiffed by paying higher premiums than you should.

The pricing of options is determined by several factors.

The Value of the Asset

The effect this has on options prices is straightforward. If the value of this asset goes down then exercising the option to sell becomes more valuable while the right to buy becomes less valuable.

On the other hand, if the value increases, the right to sell it becomes less valuable while the right to buy it becomes more appealing due to this increase.

The Intrinsic Value

When an options trader pays a premium, this sum represents two values. The premium is made up of the intrinsic value, which is the current value of the option and the potential increase in value that this option can obtain over time. This potential increase over time is known as the time value.

The intrinsic value is how much money the option is currently worth. It represents what the buyer would receive if he or she decided to exercise the option at the current time.

Intrinsic value is calculated by determining the difference in the current price of an asset and the strike price of the option.

For an option to have an intrinsic value of zero, the option must be out of money. Therefore, the buyer would not exercise the option because this would result in a loss. The common strategy here is allowing the option to expire so that no payoff is made. As a result, the intrinsic value results in nothing to the buyer.

For a buyer to be in the money, the intrinsic value has to be greater than the premium to increase the value of the option. This places the buyer in a position to make a profit. The intrinsic value of for in the money for call options and put options are calculated slightly differently. The formulas are as follows:

In the money call options:

Price of Asset - Strike Price = Intrinsic Value

In the money put option:

Strike Price - Price of Asset = Intrinsic Value

The Time Value

This value is the additional amount an investor is willing to contribute to the premium of an option in addition to the intrinsic value. This willingness stems from the belief that an option will increase in value before the expiration date reaches. Typically, an investor is only willing to put forth this extra amount if the option expires months away. There would be little to no change in the value of an option in a few days.

The time value is calculated by finding the difference between the intrinsic value of an option and the premium. The formula looks like this:

Option Premium - Intrinsic Value = Time Value

Therefore, the total price of an option premium follows this formula:

Intrinsic Value + Time Value = Option Premium

Both time value and intrinsic value help traders understand the value of what they are paying for if they decide to purchase an option. While the intrinsic value represents the worth of the option if the buyer were to exercise it at the current time, the time value represents the possible future value before or on the expiration date. These two values are important because they help traders understand the risk versus the reward of considering an option.

Volatility

This describes how likely a price change will occur during a specified amount of time on the financial market. If a financial market is nonvolatile then the prices change very slowly or remain unaffected over a specific amount of time. Volatile markets, on the other hand, have fast-changing prices over short periods.

Options traders can make use of a financial market's volatility to get a higher yield for their investment in the future. Options traders normally avoid slow-changing financial markets because these non-volatile markets often mean that no potential profit is available to the trader. Therefore, options traders thrive on volatility even though volatility increases the risk of option trading. As a result, an options trader needs to know how to read the financial market correctly to know which options are likely to yield the highest returns. This ability comes with experience, continuous learning, and keeping up to date on the happenings of the financial markets.

Many factors affect the volatility of the financial market. These factors include politics, national economics, and news reports. Options traders typically use one of two options strategies to gain the best yield from volatile markets. They are called the straddle strategy and the strangle strategy.

Interest Rates

Most people are familiar with the term interest rates. Interest rates apply to mortgages bank accounts and more. Interest rates as it applies to option trading is slightly different from the common variations.

The interest rate is defined as the percentage of a particular rate for the use of money lent over a period. This interest rate of an option has different effects on the call option and put option. The premiums for call options rise when interest rates rise and fall when interest rates fall. The effect is the opposite of put options. The premiums for put options fall when interest rates rise and rise when interest rates fall.

Interest rates affect the time value of options no matter what category they fall in.

You will come across the term risk-free interest rate many times in your study of options trading. This is described as the return made on an investment with no loss of capital. This is a misleading term because all investments carry some level of risk, no matter how minute. This more serves as a parameter in options pricing models such as the Black-Scholes model to determine the premium that should be paid.

Dividends

Dividends are distributions of portions of a company's profit at a specified period. This distribution must be decided and managed by the board of directors of a company. It is paid to a particular class of shareholders. Dividends can be distributed in the form of cash, shares of stock, and other types of property. Exchange-traded funds and mutual funds also pay out dividends.

As it relates to options trading, options do not actually pay dividends. However, the associated assets attached to that option can have them and thus, an options trader can receive those dividends if he or she exercises that option and takes ownership of those particular assets. While both call and put options can be affected by the presence of dividends of the associated asset, this effect on the types of options is widely varied. While the presence of dividends makes call options less expensive due to the anticipation of a price drop, it makes put options more expensive because the price will be decreased by the amount of the dividend.

Option Pricing Models

Option pricing theory uses all of the variables mentioned above to theoretically calculate the value of an option. It is a tool that allows trainers to get an estimate of an option's fair value as they incorporate different strategies to maximize profitability. Luckily, there are models that traders can use to implement option pricing strategies to their advantage. Three commonly used pricing models for option values are:

- The Black-Scholes Model
- Binomial Option Pricing Model
- Monte-Carlo Simulations

The Black Scholes Model

Also known as the Black-Scholes-Merton (BSM) model, this pricing model won a Nobel Prize in economics because of its effectiveness. It was designed by the three economists, Fischer Black, Robert Merton, and Myron Scholes in 1973. Originally used to price European options (meaning the option can only be exercised on the expiration date), this is a mathematical system that has a huge influence on modern option pricing. The pricing model helps differentiate options from gambling by determining the option premium to be paid logically. It calculates the return on the income the investor is likely to earn less than the amount paid.

As this is primarily used to determine a European call option, the formula used to calculate it looks like this:

SN (d1) – Xe - rt N (d2) = Call Option Premium

The letter representations in this equation stand for:

S – Current asset price

N – A normal distribution

X – Strike price

r – risk-free interest rate

t – Time of maturity

While this pricing system is great, it does have limitations. One of these limitations is that it assumes that factors like volatility and risk-free interest will remain constant, which is not the case in actuality. It also does not factor in other costs in setting up the option.

Binomial Option Pricing Model

More commonly used to develop pricing for American options, this pricing system was developed in 1979. Even as popular as the Black Scholes Model is, this model is even more frequently used in practice because it is more intuitive. This pricing system allows the assumption that there are two possible outcomes—one where the outcome moves up and one where the outcome moves down.

This system differs from the Black Scholes Model in that it allows calculations for multiple periods whereas the Black Scholes Model does not. This advantage gives a multi-period view, which is very advantageous to options traders.

This model makes use of binomial trees to figure out options pricing. These are diagrams with the main formula branching off into two different directions. This branching is what gives the multi-period view that this pricing system is famous for.

For this pricing system to work, the following assumptions are made:

- There are 2 possible prices for the associated asset, hence the name of the pricing system. Bi means 2.
- The 2 possibilities involve the price of the asset moving up or down.
- No dividends are being paid on the asset.
- The rate of interest does not change through the life of the option
- There are no risks attached to the transaction.
- There are no other costs associated with the option.

Clearly, just like with the Black Scholes Model, there is some limitation with those assumptions. Still, the pricing system is highly valuable in the valuing of American options since such options can be exercised at any time until the expiration date.

Monte Carlo Simulations

Used in multiple fields across the board like science, engineering, and finance, this model allows the options trader to consider multiple outcomes due to the involvement of random factors. It allows for the consideration of risk and unpredictability, unlike the first two pricing models. This is why it is also sometimes called multiple probability simulation.

A Final Word on Pricing

The reason I went into such depth on pricing options is that I want you to realize that everything related to options requires careful consideration right down to the premiums paid. This needs to be a fair trade for all the parties involved and premium pricing needs to reflect that fairness. When considering the options premium, remember to search deeper than the surface level to ensure that fairness and to ensure that you are gaining the profit that you need out of the transaction.

Chapter 9: How to Choose the Strike Price for Options Trading

The strike price of an option is the price at which a put or call option can be exercised. It is otherwise called the exercise price. Picking the strike price is one of two key choices (the other being time to expiration) a financial specialist or trader must make while choosing a specific option. The strike price has a tremendous bearing on how your options trading will play out.

Strike Price Considerations

Accept that you have identified the stock on which you need to make an options exchange. Your subsequent stage is to pick an options strategy, for example, purchasing a call or composing a put. Then, the two most significant considerations in deciding the strike price are your hazard resistance and your ideal hazard reward result.

Hazard Tolerance

Suppose you are thinking about purchasing a call choice. Your hazard resilience ought to decide if you picked an in-the-money (ITM) call option, an at-the-money (ATM) call, or an out-of-the-money (OTM) call. An ITM choice has a higher affectability—otherwise called the option delta—to the price of the fundamental stock. If the stock price increments by a given sum, the ITM call would acquire than an ATM or OTM call. Be that as it may, if the stock value decays, the higher delta of the ITM option additionally implies, it would diminish over an ATM or OTM call if the price of the fundamental stock falls.

Hazard Reward Payoff

Your ideal hazard reward result uses methods that measure the capital you need to chance on the exchange and your anticipated benefit target. An ITM call might be less dangerous than an OTM call; however, it costs more. If you just need to bet a modest quantity of capital on your call exchange thought, the OTM call might be the best, pardon the joke, option.

An OTM call can have a lot bigger increase in rate terms than an ITM call if the stock's floods past the strike price; however, it has a significantly less possibility of achievement than an ITM call. That implies, even though you plunk down a little measure of money to purchase an OTM call, the chances you may lose everything of your venture are higher than with an ITM call.

Given these considerations, a relatively conservative financial specialist may choose an ITM or ATM call. Then again, a dealer with high resilience for hazard may incline toward an OTM call. The models in the accompanying area illustrate a portion of these ideas.

Picking the Wrong Strike Price

If you are a call or a put purchaser, picking an inappropriate strike price may bring about the loss of the full premium paid. These hazard increments when the strike price is set further out of the money. On account of a call essayist, an inappropriate strike price for the shrouded call may bring about the fundamental stock being called away. A few speculators want to compose somewhat OTM calls. That gives them a better yield if the stock is called away, even though it implies sacrificing some top-notch gains.

For a put trader, an inappropriate strike price would bring about the hidden stock being relegated at prices well over the present market price. That may happen if the stock dives unexpectedly, or if there is an abrupt market auction, sending most offer prices forcefully lower.

Strike Price Points to Consider

The strike price is an essential segment of making productive options play. There are numerous interesting points as you calculate this value level.

Have a Backup Plan

Options trading necessitates a considerably more active methodology than commonplace purchase and-hold contributing. Have a management plan prepared for your options trading, on the off chance that there is an abrupt swing in sentiment for a specific stock or in the wide market.

Time rot can quickly disintegrate the value of your long choice positions. Think about cutting your misfortunes and moderating venture capital if things are not going in your direction.

Evaluate Different Payoff Scenarios

You ought to have an approach for different situations if you plan to exchange options effectively. For instance, if you consistently compose secured calls, what are the reasonable adjustments if the stocks are called away, as opposed to not called? Assume that you are bullish on a stock.

Would it be progressively beneficial to purchase short-dated options at a lower strike price, or longer-dated options at a higher strike price?

The Bottom Line

Picking the strike price is a key decision for an option's financial specialist or trader since it has a significant effect on the gainfulness of an option. Getting your work done to choose the ideal strike price is an essential advance to improve your odds of success in options trading.

Chapter 10: Credit and Debit Spreads Options

Credit Spread

Most options traders that make money doing options trading for income do it by selling put options. The goal is basically to pick a strike price that is low enough, so the probability of the put option going in the money is remote. For level three traders, using a put credit spread is the method of selling put options. It involves buying and selling a put option simultaneously. But in this case, we are going to set up the trade so that the higher strike put option is the one that we sell.

Then you are going to choose a lower-priced put option to buy. This is going to mitigate the risk, but the type of risk we are mitigating when selling a credit spread is different than the kind of risk we have thought about mitigating to this point.

First off, let's clarify when you would enter into a put credit spread. This is a trade that you will enter when you think that the price of the stock will stay the same, or it will rise. We can add to this and say that it's even OK if the stock price drops, but you want it to avoid dropping too much. This can all be encapsulated by saying that we only hope that the share price will stay higher than the put option's strike price that you sell. Otherwise, you don't care a whit what the stock price does.

As a part of the trade, the put option is bought at the same time with a lower strike price. Since the strike price is lower, it will cost less than the amount that you received from selling the high priced put option. Therefore, there is a net credit for the transaction, which is the gained premium for selling the put option with the high price of the strike, minus the premium payment for buying the put option with the low strike price. This transaction is carried out in a single trade. Many brokers will have some put credit spreads already set up for you, so you don't have to do anything but enter into the trade.

Let's get a clear understanding of how this works. Furthermore, we need to note that you are not going to have to buy any stocks; the stocks are bought and sold on your behalf automatically by the broker if this occurs.

The lower strike price put option is going to cap the possible losses incurred by having to buy the shares of stock. The way this is going to work out is if the stock drops by a large amount, you are going to have shares put to you at the higher strike price, meaning that you are going to have to buy the shares at that high price. But then you will be able to turn around and put the shares to the seller of the lower strike price put option so that you don't have to pay full price.

Let's look at a specific example to see how it would work. Also, remember that you have to factor in the breakeven price of the put options. So, if the price of the share falls lower than the price of the strike of the higher put, it has to drop below the price strike less the paid premium for that option. Otherwise, the option is not going to be exercised because the other party to the trade would lose money.

Now, let's create a hypothetical example that illustrates the concepts.

We will use Apple to see how this works. We can sell a $230 put (with the share price at $236) for $410. That is $4.10 a share. Therefore, the breakeven price would be $230 - $4.10 = $225.90. The share price is going to have to drop below $225.90 before any trader would consider exercising this option. Since it's a put option, exercising means that, as the seller of the option, you would be forced to buy 100 shares of stock. For a hypothetical example, suppose that the share price had dropped to $224 a share. This would be done at the strike price. So, the total cost would be 100 x $230 = $23,000. In this case, you could sell the shares on the open market for $22,400. So, your total loss would be $600.

If you didn't buy a put option to offset the risk, this means you would be open, at least in theory, for much larger losses. Say the stock price dropped to $190. In that case, you could still sell the shares after being forced to buy them when the put option was exercised, but you would have to sell them for $19,000. So, your loss, in this case, would be $4,000.

The way a put credit spread works is you buy a put option to prevent this kind of loss. For example, you can buy a put option with a strike price of $225 for $253, or $2.35 a share. So the way that things work out, in this case, is that if the share price drops below $225 to $190, to use as our example, since you bought the second put option, you would be able to sell the 100 shares you were forced to buy at $230 a share for $225 a share. Your total loss would be $5 a share, the difference between the two strike prices, for a total loss of $500. But we have to subtract the net credit for that, which is $4.10 - $2.53 = $1.57. So, the risk mitigation would limit the total loss to $500 - $157 = $343.

You can earn substantial income selling put credit spreads. You can increase your income by selling multiple put credit spreads simultaneously, or you can aim for high priced stocks. For example, consider GOOG (Google, which has a share price of $1,243). Choosing strike prices of $1242.50 and $1227.50, you can earn $545 as long as the options expire with the share price higher than the higher strike price. The maximum possible loss, in this case, would be $955.

The longer the expiration date, the more money that can be earned. Considering Amazon, which has a share price of $1,769, with a six-month time to expiration, you can earn $3,765, provided that the share price stays above $1,685.

Debit Spread

The key to long-term options trading is to get level three trading status. Once you have done this, many new strategies will become available that will significantly increase your odds of making profits.

A call debit spread involves two options in the same trade. You are going to buy one call option, and then you are going to sell a call option. The trade is entered into using one step, so you are not going to be focused on selling a call option. You simply pick the two options you want to use, and then you tell the broker which one to buy and which one to sell, and they take care of everything for you.

Then an option should be sold with the price of the strike that is higher. The strike price option that is higher is used to put a cap on your potential losses. Let's see how this works.

For the sake of example, say you trade a stock per share that costs $200. Let's say that you buy a call option with a $195 strike price for $500. If you only did this, your potential loss is $500.

But you can reduce the loss by selling a second call option in the same trade, creating a call debit spread. You pick a second call option that has a $202 price of the strike. For example, we will say that you can sell this for $250 (prices are for illustration only). Now, you have capped the possible loss to $250, cutting it in half.

The premium you receive for selling the $202 strike is yours to keep, so no matter what happens, that mitigates the losses. Potential profit occurs when the share price stays above the strike price of the lower strike used in the trade, which is $195 for our hypothetical example. The higher it goes above this value, the more profit you earn until you get to the higher strike of $202. From this point onward, the amount of profit earned is capped.

For a call debit spread, you calculate the net debit for the transaction. That will be the price paid per share of the call option you buy, less the price received per share of the option you sell. Then the breakeven price is the option's strike price you buy, plus the net debit for the transaction. So, if you have a net debit of $6.82 for a call debit spread with a $240 lower price of a strike, the price of the breakeven is $246.82.

Max gain is reached when the share price reaches the price of the strike of the option that has a higher price in the pair that you sold, and it is fixed for any share price that goes above that value. Call debit spreads work like calls but allows you to earn limited, fixed profits.

Put Debit Spread

The same type of strategy can be used with put options. In this case, we obtain a put debit spread. The numbers are simply reverse. The first part of a put debit spread is buying a put option with a higher strike price. This is where you hope to make your profits. Then, you will sell a put option that has a lower strike price to help mitigate your risk. The premium received from selling the put option, although it will be smaller than the premium paid to buy the put option with the higher strike price, will help you to reduce the potential losses if the trade does not work out.

The price paid for the higher strike price put less the price received for selling; the lower strike price put will give you the net debit for the trade. The breakeven price, in this case, is found by taking the higher strike price and then subtracting the net debit. Profits are obtained when the price of the stock falls to or less than the breakeven price. When the price of the stock reaches the lower price of the strike, then the maximum profit happens. It is constant from there, despite how little the price of the stock drops.

A put debit spread helps you to mitigate your overall risk, at the expense of limiting your possible profits. If you had one put option, the potential earnings are obtained if the stock were to drop to zero. For example, if we bought an Apple put option with a price of a strike of $225, you could earn 100 x $225 = $22,500, if Apple stock was completely wiped out. Of course, that is a very unlikely scenario, but we describe it to give you an idea of what is theoretically possible for earnings when you invest in a put option. However, if we were to sell a put option as a part of the same trade with a strike price of $205, our gains would be capped at $1,415. That is a substantial profit, but even if the stock drops to $100 a share, $50 a share, or even $0 a share, we would only make $1,415. That is a good example that shows you how debit spreads work.

Chapter 11: Iron Condor Options

Do you know that iron condor is something you want to apply when the highs and lows of stock prices seem to be bounded? It is as if the stock price is trapped. It never breaks above a certain pricing level, called resistance. But it never drops below a given price level, which is called support. Sometimes a stock can be trapped in this pattern for a long period.

To have support and resistance, you want to see the price touch the line of support at least two times, and the line of resistance at least two times. The difference in prices might be relatively small. Of course, there are some possibilities for trading calls and puts; when the price drops down to the support level, you can buy call options and take profit as the price goes back up toward the resistance price level. Then you can buy put options and sell them when the price drops back down to support.

Option Trader

This type of options trader seeks to minimize risk and set up trades so that they can earn a regular income from the markets. There are many different ways to do this, and most of them involve selling rather than buying options. When you are a regular options trader, you buy to open your positions. So, you are going to be running your business buying low and selling high to make profits.

Income traders sell to open their positions. They seek to make money selling options, and while you have been concerned about things like theta and time decay so far. As an income trader, your value time decays, and can't wait for options to expire.

An iron condor is the first type of strategy that we are going to consider that works in this fashion. When you trade an iron condor, you are going to sell it to open your position. Then you are going to make money from the time decay. As long as the stock stays within the range that you use to define the iron condor, you will earn a profit. If it moves outside the range of the iron condor, then you are going to lose money.

A single iron condor isn't going to make you a huge amount of money. The basic philosophy behind it is that this is a limited risk—limited profit type of trade. It eliminates having to guess which direction the stock is going to move, and instead, we are only going to estimate the bounds of stock price movement over the lifetime of the option. Under normal conditions, this type of bet is going to work in most cases. Of course, if there is unexpected news, such as bad news coming out about the company that can cause prices to move outside the bounds of the iron condor and turn the trade into a loser. The unexpectedly bad news about the economy or political situation can have the same effect.

To create an iron condor, we are going to trade four options at once. We are going to sell two options and buy two options. First, let's look at the high price range for the trade. We want to sell a call option with a lower strike price. The strike price used for the call option sets the upper boundary of the iron condor. So, you are setting this up with the belief that the stock price is not going to exceed the strike price of the call option that you select.

Second, we are going to buy a call option that has a higher strike price than the first call option. This is done because we are going to use it to hedge our risks a little bit. Let's see how that would work. For our example, we will assume that the stock price is $200.

We could sell a call option with a strike price of $205. This means we are setting up our iron condor with the belief that from now until the expiration date of the option, the price of the stock is not going to rise above $205. If there are 30 days to expiration, and volatility is a relatively low 15%, the price of a call option with a $205 strike price is going to be $1.55.

The breakeven price is found by adding the cost of the call option to the strike price, which would give $206.55. As long as the share price stays at $206.55 or below, it's not worth it for the option to be exercised. However, if the share price goes above that value, the option can be exercised. In the case of a call option, as the options seller, this means that you have to sell 100 shares of stock at the strike price of $205 a share.

So how would that work in practice? The way it works is your broker buys the shares at the market price, sells the shares to the counterparty to the option contract to close the transaction at the lower strike price, and then they stick you with the losses. So, if the share price was $208, you would have a $3 loss per share or a total loss of $300 for each contract that would cover 100 shares of stock.

Of course, stock prices can rise to any value, at least in theory. So, you could be getting into real trouble if the stock price rose much higher. The iron condor caps maximum losses by including a second call option, with a higher strike price. You buy this call option, which means you cap possible profits because you have this added expense. But besides limiting possible profits, it will also cap possible losses.

Since you are buying a call option, you can exercise your rights on that option and buy shares of stock at that strike price that you can sell at the higher market price to make up for some of the loss.

Using our price setup, we could choose $210 as the second-strike price. Suppose that the stock price rises to $212. In this situation, the first option with the $205 strike price is going to be exercised. So, we have to buy shares at $212 and then sell them to the counterparty of the $205 option at $205 a share, giving us a net loss of $7 a share.

But now we can exercise the second call option that we have purchased. In this case, we buy shares of stock at $210, but then we sell them on the market for $212, giving us a net of $2 a share. This helps mitigate the total losses, reducing the total loss to $5 a share, or a total loss of $500. The loss is capped. It's going to be the difference between the two strike prices chosen for our options.

The options that you sell are the ones that set the boundaries for the iron condor. In this case, we have the call option with a strike price of $205 and a put option with a strike price of $195. That means as long as the stock price stays between $195 and $205 among the time, we sell to open this position, and when the options expire, we will earn a profit.

In addition to selling a put option, we will attempt to mitigate risk in the same way that we did with our setup of the call options. This means that we are going to buy a put option with a lower strike price to set the final lower boundary for the iron condor. Again, it can be any value, but for the sake of clarity, we will put it at the same $5 distance.

Now let's take a look at what would happen if the stock price went outside the range we have set up to the downside. We have sold a put option with a strike price of $195 and purchased a put option with a strike price of $190. If the share price of the stock falls below $195 but remains above $190, the put option that we sold can be exercised. When a put option is exercised, that means that we will be forced to buy shares of stock at the strike price. So, we have to buy shares at $195 a share even though the price on the market is between $190 and $195, let's say for the sake of example, it's $192. We then have to sell the shares at the market price. So, if we sell the shares for $192, we are out $3 a share for a total loss of $3 a share.

If the stock price kept dropping, we would find ourselves with ever-increasing losses. But that is why we buy the second put option; it serves the same purpose as the second call option in mitigating our losses. So, if the share price drops to say $170, our losses will be capped at the difference between the strike prices of the two put options. Instead of being forced to sell the shares at the market price of $170 a share, we would be able to exercise the second put option and sell the shares at $190 a share. So, we had to buy them at $195 a share even though the market price was $170 a share, but then we can sell them to someone else for $190 a share.

Let's see what the prices are for each of the options in this case:

$210 Call Option (BUY): $0.57

$205 Call Option (SELL): $1.55

$195 Put Option (SELL): $1.45

$190 Put Option (BUY): $0.47

The cost of buying the two options is $0.57 + $0.47 = $1.04. But we receive a credit from selling the other two options of $1.55 + $1.45 = $3. Our net credit is $3 - $1.04 = $1.96.

We start ahead by $1.96. So, if we end up losing on the trade because the stock breaks one way or another, our losses, which were already capped at $5, are reduced by this amount, and so our total possible loss in any situation is $5 - $1.96 = $3.04. That means the maximum possible loss is $304 (for a total of 100 shares), and the maximum profit, which is fixed, is $196.

In the example we've deliberated so far, the losses seem to outstrip the gains. However, that is a deceiving way to look at the trade. With an iron condor, the probability of winning on the trade—provided that you've done your homework and picked stock in a low volatility situation—is high. The key to succeeding with an iron condor is carefully studying and choosing your trades. Don't just randomly pick a stock and then enter an iron condor.

Buying Back to Close

One strategy people use is they buy back the iron condor to close the position. You can choose to do this or not. The reason you would do it would be if there is a possibility of the stock breaking one way or the other, and then you would be put in a position of having the options that you sold exercised.

You can trade iron condors on different time frames. The longer you select for your time frame, the longer you are going to have to wait for either time decay to work well enough for you to buy it back and still make a profit, or for you to let it expire and make the maximum profit.

Chapter 12: Leverage of Options

The process of using borrowed capital (debt) to increase the shareholder's return on their investments or equity in capital structure is called financial leverage or Trading on equity. The financial leverage analyzed by the firm is intended to earn more return on the fixed charge funds rather than their costs. The surplus will increase the return on the owner's equity, whereas the deficit will decrease the return on the owner's equity. Financial leverage affects the EPS (Earnings per share). When the EBIT increases, then EPS increases.

For example, if the firm borrows a debt from creditors for $1000 at 7% interest per annum, i.e., $70, and invests this debt to earn a 12% return on this, i.e., $120 per annum. Then the difference of surplus, i.e., $50, which is after interest payment made to the creditors of the firm, will belong to the shareholders or owners of the firm, and it is referred to as profit from financial leverage. Conversely, if the firm would earn a 5% return, then the firm has a loss of $20 (i.e., $70 - $50) to the shareholders.

Highly leveraged companies may be at risk of bankruptcy if they are unable to make a payment on their debt, but it can increase shareholder's return on their investment, and there are tax advantages associated with leverage.

Financial leverage ratio = EBIT / EBT

The financial leverage ratio is used to analyze the Capital structure and financial risk of the company. It explains how the fixed interest-bearing loan capital affects the operating profit of the firm. If EBIT is more than EBT, this ratio becomes more than 1. A slightly higher ratio is favorable, i.e., if this ratio is marginally more than 1 that is nearer to 1, it indicates moderate use of debt capital, low financial risk, and good financial judgment.

Why is Leverage Riskier?

Another significant risk to be aware of is that of leverage. Because Options don't cost much as stock as they are simply a contract, this means that they experience disproportionately larger percentage price gains in reaction to the far more expensive underlying stock's very small price movements. The huge benefit of this is that it results in large percentage gains when the underlying stock moves in the anticipated direction by even a small amount. The downside, though, is that it also results in a 100% wipe-out of the investment if the stock moves by even the smallest amount in the wrong direction. This is not necessarily an issue with beginners, or at least it shouldn't be as the risk manifests itself mainly through trading too large a position size. However, you need to be aware that as beneficial as leverage is, it can also be a double-edged sword, so be aware that leverage is a risk that needs to be addressed. One simple way to nullify or minimize this level of risk is to keep your position size small.

Lastly, Options, as we know, possesses a time value (extrinsic value) in addition to their inherent intrinsic value (in the money value), which is also another double-edged sword. For option buyers, time-decay acts as a headwind because it is continually decreasing the value of the option. By doing so, increases the dependency on greater stock price movement to break even on the trade. For option writers, it acts as a tailwind because it allows a profit to be generated through steady premium incomes regardless of whether the stock moves or not.

The Advantages of Leverage in Options Trading

The options exchanges play a critical role in ensuring that there are enough securities to base options contracts on. Following are some of the significant functions of an options exchange.

Liquidity

Perhaps the biggest function of options exchanges is to ensure ready markets for options contracts. The markets ensure that holders of options can exercise their options and that there are enough buyers to purchase the options. Traders are looking for avenues to increase their earning potential, and liquidity helps them achieve that. Options contracts have a time limit, unlike other securities such as shares, which necessitates liquidity. The existence of market makers is particularly responsible for liquidity.

Gauging a Country's Economy

The state of an options market can reliably inform us what the country's economic situation is like. The most common underlying assets that traders base their options on our shares. The prevailing economic conditions are always reflected in the share prices of various companies. If the country is experiencing prosperity, the share prices will be up, and if the country is experiencing market crashes, the share prices will go down. Thus, the options exchanges play a critical role in ensuring that traders have a sense of how their country is performing economy-wise. Stocks are the pulse of an economy, and they are accurate predictors of a country's economic state.

Securities Pricing

Options traders have a wide pool to choose from when it comes to underlying assets. However, the value of an underlying asset is determined by the options exchange according to the forces of demand and supply. The financial securities of prosperous companies are worth more than the securities of moderately successful companies. The valuation of securities is important not only for traders but also for governments. Governments levy taxes on earnings drawn from options trading, so they first have to get the value of the securities.

Safety of Transactions

Traders want to be sure that they can trust all the parties that they are getting into business with. Therefore, it is the work of an options exchange to ensure the players are trustworthy. For one, most options contracts are based on financial securities of publicly listed companies, and these companies must operate within stringent rules and regulations. Thus, the trader is assured of security when dealing with other parties. The options markets should provide all relevant information about options contracts and securities to discourage the trader from making a move out of ignorance.

Providing Speculation Scope

Speculation of securities is critical to ensure a healthy balance of demand and supply of securities. Many traders earn their profits from purely speculative risk. They have developed a skill of determining the movement of prices. The options exchanges provide traders with the resources and tools of speculating on the securities performance, thus allowing traders to earn profits.

Promotes an Investment Culture

Options exchanges are critical in promoting the culture of investing in valuable securities like the stock as opposed to unproductive assets such as precious metals. Traders have a wide selection of underlying securities to base their options contracts on; thus, they are not limited in the range of their strategies. A strong saving and investment culture is critical for the economic advancement of a country.

The Continuous Market for Securities

Options exchanges allow traders to base their options on a wide range of underlying securities, and in case of any risks, traders are at liberty to switch from one security to the subsequent. This is different from purchasing stocks wherein you are stuck with the consequences of poor decisions.

Capital Formation

Options exchanges promote the pooling together and redistribution of resources. The exchanges create a win-win situation for both sides. Companies raise capital when their stocks are publicly listed, and their securities act as the underlying. On the other hand, traders stand to benefit from the high earning potential and low-capital requirements for options contracts. So, options exchanges play a critical role in ensuring that the parties are in a position to generate capital.

Control Companies

The significance of transparency within the derivatives market cannot be overstated. If a trader has the misfortune of working with shady companies, they could easily lose their earnings. Options exchanges make it hard for shady companies to spoil the market. For instance, publicly-traded companies have to submit relevant documents and adhere to certain performance standards, as doing so will boost investor confidence. Companies that refuse to cooperate with exchanges are blacklisted from the market.

Fiscal and Monetary Policies

The fiscal policy and the monetary policy of the government must not hurt the players in the financial industry. Options exchanges facilitate the creation and execution of key policies that will govern the financial markets.

Proper Canalization of Wealth

Options are a great way of putting capital into greater use, as opposed to having the capital just sitting around. Thus, the economy benefits from an injection of capital, which would otherwise have been inactive. The injection of capital into the economy promotes wealth distribution and fights off economic disgraces like unemployment.

Education Purposes

Options trading features complex processes. Even people who claim to understand options trading might be low-key deluded. Thus, the importance of education cannot be overstated. Many traders just get the hang of things and set about purchasing and selling options contracts, forgetting that it is critical first to educate one's self. Options exchanges provide a wealth of resources and information that are meant to enlighten traders. Empowered traders improve trading activity.

Disadvantages of Leverage in Options Trading

Again, I won't bore you with elaborate explanations of the disadvantages of options trading. Instead, here's another helpful list that clearly outlines why traders might choose to shy away from potential options trading opportunities:

- Options are time-sensitive investments. Yes, you can pick and choose options based on expiration dates, but you'll always be confined to a certain expiration date where you must choose to act or choose to exit.

- Successful options trading requires your attention and time. Without it, you risk losing out on potential profit-generating opportunities that come from buying or selling your call or put option at the right, most profitable time.

- Options are without a paper-trail. With stocks and bonds, for example, you'll receive some sort of paper certification regarding your investment. Options are "book-entry" investments, meaning you receive no paper certification that shows your claim to an option or your ownership of an option.

- You're working in the stock market, a highly volatile place where changes occur suddenly and dramatically. You'll need to be on constant alert, or at least hire a broker who will.

- You'll need to be in a somewhat stable financial situation before you can successfully trade. Establishing and frequently adding to some sort of "trading fund" before you begin your options, trading endeavors will somewhat remedy an unstable financial situation, however.

Chapter 13: Which Options Trading Platform to Use

A vital aspect of options trading is the platform that one uses to trade. This is because options trading requires monitoring and requires a continuous analysis of trends. Performance is also monitored, and since the trade is impacted upon by a complex of factors, one must choose a suitable platform for trading.

A good platform should offer a lot of opportunities for traders. These are opportunities to orient beginners into trading, development for the existing ones, and actualization for those with a record on the platform. Such a platform should also prescribe the available products and any resources that subscribers on the platform can benefit from to push themselves to profitability.

With the technology developing at high speed, platforms continue to improve by the day. This is both complicating the trading itself as well as providing avenues of spreading awareness about the business. A platform should have the ability to offer the best possible experience for the traders to do trade and grow both in experience and returns without meeting a lot of platform limitations and frustrations.

A Platform Takes Trading to the Holders

Trading involves a lot of complexities that may sometimes be scary. It makes people lose interest as soon as they develop it. They perceive it as too complicated. The impression is that it is a venture meant for the people who have higher comprehension of concepts in the economics specialty and that those who do not a background in this area will have difficulty getting on board.

A trading platform needs to present options trading as a venture that is possible and in which anyone with interest can succeed. The days when options trading and any other forms of trading were presented as a show of sophistication are long gone. In this era, every sector of investment is portrayed as conceivable, and businesses are now being made easier to create a better chance for people to dare. A platform that limits investment so much and is exclusive in terms of how it carries out its trading activities is irrelevant to modern economic patterns.

Platforms, thus, have to be interactive and user-friendly. They should have the ability to encourage users to feel like they can handle the trade. It should also have the capability to gauge the level of use and give feedback about how well they can use it. If it's a website, for instance, it should report the numbers as people visit it and how many eventually end up creating accounts and trading. Counting traffic is essential for feedback that can lead to the creation of a better experience for the users.

Competition

In choosing a platform sometimes, one would want to take advantage of the advantages of different platforms. This is looking at one's style of trading and how they wish to monitor their business and see if a platform is more transparent in handling the tares or whether it offers a clear lens of controlling purchases and sales of options. This is the reason why the various platforms must be assessed in terms of their potential. Usually, platforms are related to the tools of trading. Some of the tools of trading can be found right on the platform of trading.

When a platform of trading also has various tools of aiding trading, it ensures that one can gain a lot of benefits in one place. This makes the platform a utility where a person can visit for more purposes than just trading. It also makes it better. For instance, if a platform has videos that offer trading tutorials. This can make it resourceful in imparting competency in participating in the very sector that the platform operates.

To best benefit from competition, one should understand the type of trade they want to do. This is by naming their price and gauging which platform can serve better in ensuring returns and value generation. This is to avoid going into trading in desperation, and one has to be patient to see if the platform can also come out and meet a trader at their point of ability and also help in trading in comfort where risk is at a minimum.

Types of Trading Platforms

There are various platforms in options trading that one could consider. There is web-based trading that utilizes the power of the search engines. This platform has many operators since the building of websites in the modern age is easy. This is responsible for the growth in the popularity of options trading. People can trade with anyone, open brokerage accounts, make deposits, and participate in the buying and selling of assets in the comfort of their homes.

With the presence of a lot of technological gadgets such as smartphones, tablets, and computers, web-based trading has been easy and within reach. Websites can be built with additional resources for learning and tools that can be an advantage for both novice and seasoned traders. On the websites, regular updates on the market can be posted to keep traders informed about trends, patterns, and even help in analyzing price movements for the subscribers.

The web is also a good platform when it comes to filtering opportunities and options based on suitability and preferences given the various abilities of users. They can be designed to be customizable even when the options markets are standardized.

User Friendliness

Friendliness is also in terms of the efforts that are made to create peer assistance. This is through creating groups of traders that influence each other and can learn from the vast experiences in the trading of the options. This can be a positive influence on the journey to gaining competence and help support an environment where people can relate and interact as they pursue their various financial goals.

Tools to Learn

Upon mastering the various basics of trading and making the initial moves to start trading, one will use various tools that help indicate the advancers and decliners on the market. Greeks are metrics that those involved in options trading capital to ensure maximization of returns. These "Greeks" include the delta matrix that measures the correlation between price movements of the underlying asset relative to the price of the option. The tools for monitoring the movements for these parameters of trading are vital as everyone trades with a focus on minimizing losses while geared towards profit maximization.

Some salient features of options are measured in terms called the Greeks and labeled with Greek letters. It's really essential to understand the Greeks if you're going to get serious about trading options.

- Beta: Beta, β, is a characteristic of the underlying stock and measures the historical volatility of that stock. It gives equal weight to volatility on the upside as well as on the downside. When you're evaluating a stock, you can get a sense of how variable the stock's price is by looking at the β. A stable stock that moves with the market will have a beta value of about 1. If beta is less than 1, it tends to lag the market that is a $1 movement in the market a stock with a beta less than 1 means it will increase or decrease less than $1. Conversely, a stock with a beta greater than 1 means the stock price will move more than the market, up or down. Stocks with low betas are more stable than those with a higher beta. Examples of low beta are utilities. Stocks with a high beta include industries like biotechnology.

- Vega: Vega is a measure of the volatility of the option price. The option price is related to the underlying stock price, but the option price is also variable. Vega is a measure of that volatility, but it's an implied volatility, not a historical volatility as is beta. Vega is the only Greek trading term without a Greek letter symbol.

- Delta: Delta, δ, measures the change in the price of an option in response to a change in the price of the underlying stock. For example, if an option has a Delta of 0.45, when the underlying stock changes by $1, the option will change by $0.45.

- Gamma: Gamma, γ, measures the rate of change in the underlying stock, not the change itself. Gamma expresses how fast the option responds to changes in Delta. Gamma is expressed as a positive or negative number. A positive gamma indicates that changes in the delta will be correlated with positive movements in the underlying stock. A negative gamma has the opposite indication.

- Theta: Theta, θ, measures how much value the option will lose as days pass until expiration comes. The loss is due primarily to the time value of money. As a wasting asset, an option's value will decline because of the concept behind time value. A dollar today is worth more than a dollar next week. This time decay is difficult to calculate and most economic models are complex and often not particularly accurate.

Professional Level Platforms

There is a level in trading where one attains sophistication and attains the intuition to thrive in options trading regardless of the ways market forces seem to behave. At this level, someone needs tools that enable them to edge into the horizon of complexity in trading. The platforms for this professional level exist, and they have to offer tools that are an edge above the basic level. These tools have to offer strategies of competing to control the stocks and rise above the market forces. At this level, one becomes daring, and the possibilities that the platform offers should only be dared by those who have mastered trading and are sure of beating odds as they speculate about squeezing out value-form trades that otherwise be perceived as highly risky.

Mobile Trading

Mobile trading also comes to keep people abreast. This is because opportunities sometimes appear and disappear on people because they aren't using a device that enables them to be precise and timely in decision making and action.

With mobile trading, apps have been developed, some with notification capability. One can customize the apps to ensure that no opportunity comes that is not taken advantage of. Opportunities in trading must be seized and relying on a platform that is less reliable and useful means that opportunities for trading are lost.

What Are We Looking for in Platforms and Tools?

First is the opportunity to learn. There is no worse platform of trading than that which targets only to admit traders who do not understand what they are getting into. The education that a platform has to offer should be free as trading is itself risky enough to prohibit any extra expenses in the process. Platform operators should understand that anyone to visit their platform is a potential subscriber, and they should freely offer support to educate them for the acquisition of requisite knowledge on options trading.

Excellent broker services try to suit customer needs. They ask options traders on their platform what their preferred means of communication is. Whether a live chat or phone call suits the customer or not. They also dedicate a desk for trading communications and queries and have the discipline to listen to customers and their issues with patience. They, in fact, have feedback on the quality of customer service that those who reach out get.

Software Trading Platforms

These are more complex than web-based ones. This is because they are run on the trader's computer, and the trader is required to understand what the software does and interpret it. Even when the brokerage can assist, software-based platforms require the trader to have enough technical know-how to read charts, graphs, and understand patterns that represent various components of options trading.

For beginners, a complex platform is to be avoided by all means. This is because one is bound to engage in aspects of trading that they do not understand. A trading platform needs to be clear and simple. The interface should not be too busy as to scare away those traders who aren't accustomed. This is the reason why operators usually separate the platforms that as designed for basic use, which is suitable for novices, and advanced trading for the seasoned ones.

Then a broker has to offer a tutorial that guides the user on how to navigate their platform. Everything should be explained, even those that one would deem to be obvious. Screenshots can even be available to be categorical and emphatic. This ensures that a broker has offered all possible assists for the trader to benefit from the offers and products on the platform successfully.

Cost Implication

The trader needs to know that some brokers may have charges attached to some of the services, resources, and tools that they provide on their platform. These must be assessed in terms of their worth and whether the costs are necessary. Making some tolls premium may be an indicator of quality but not always. This is particularly the case when other platforms provide similar services toll-free.

Screening tools are particularly the ones that are bound to attract charges because they have abilities to analyze and assess market trends. They can think about the trader and help him in decision-making. One should read about the specifications of the tools and ascertain what they or cannot do. This is so they know if they are customizable according to the needs and conveniences of traders.

Some charges can even be attached to the quotes update feed. Usually, the quotes can be accessed in real-time for those who want to see them in real-time. The quotes are useful in influencing idea generation and sometimes can tip people of opportunities in the market. There is usually a delay for those who access the quotes updates for free.

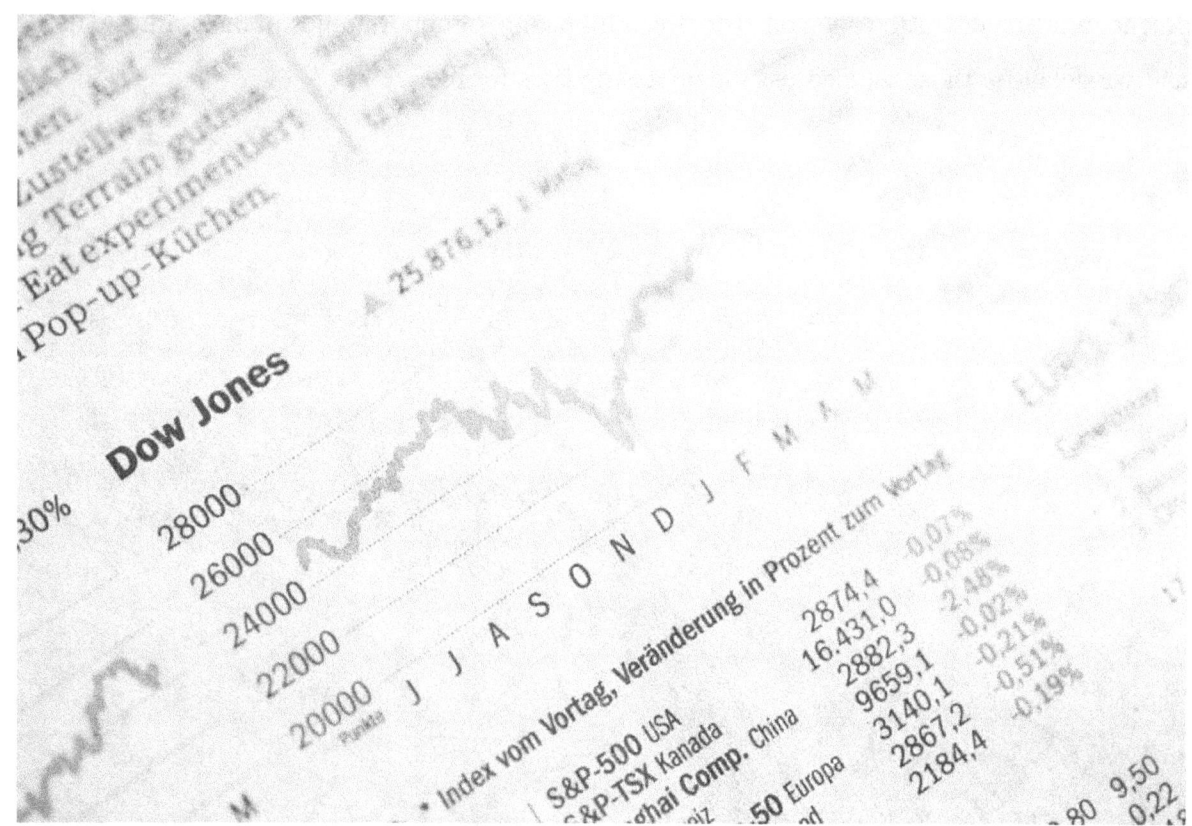

Buying OTM Call Options

As anyone might expect, these options are shabby which is as they should be. When you purchase an OTM shabby option, they don't consequently increment because the stock moves the correct way. If the move is near termination and it's insufficient to achieve the strike, the likelihood of the stock proceeding with the move in the now abbreviated period is low. Consequently, the cost of the option will mirror that likelihood.

Using the Same Strategy in different Conditions

Option exchanging is strikingly adaptable. It can empower you to trade adequately in a wide range of economic situations. Be that as it may, you can just exploit this adaptability on the off chance that you remain open to adopting new systems.

When you purchase a spread, it is otherwise called a long spread position. Every new options trader ought to acclimate themselves with the potential outcomes of spreads, so you can start to perceive the correct conditions to utilize them.

No Exit Plan before Expiration

. In exchanging options, much the same as stocks, it's essential to control your feelings. This doesn't mean gulping each dread in a super-human manner. It's significantly more straightforward than that: have the arrangement to work and work your arrangement.

Making Up for Previous Losses with Risk

Every single prepared option trader has been there. Confronting this situation, you're frequently enticed to break a wide range of individual guidelines, essentially to continue exchanging a similar option you began with. Wouldn't it be more pleasant if the whole market wasn't right, not you? As a stock trader, you've presumably heard comparative support for bending over to make up for a lost time: on the off chance that you preferred the stock at 80 when you got it, you must love it at 50. It can entice to purchase progressively and bring down the net cost premise on the trade.

Trading Non-Liquid Options

Stock markets are by and large more liquid than their related options markets for a straightforward reason: Stock traders are on the whole exchanging only one stock, however, the option traders may have many options contracts to browse. Stock traders will run to only one type of IBM stock, for instance, yet options traders for IBM have maybe six distinct lapses and plenty of strike costs to look over. More decisions by definition imply the options market will likely not be as liquid as the stock market.

Failing to Dividend Date in Strategy

It pays to monitor profit and profit dates for your hidden stock. For instance, on the off chance that you've sold calls and there's a profit drawing closer, it builds the likelihood you might be allotted early. This is particularly valid if the profit is relied upon to be expansive. That is because option proprietors have no right to a profit. To gather it, the options trader needs to practice the option and purchase the fundamental stock.

Failing If You Are Assigned Early

For instance, imagine a scenario where you're running a long call spread, and the higher-strike short option is doled out. Starting traders may frenzy and exercise the lower-strike long option with a specific end goal to convey the stock. However, that is presumably not the best choice. It's generally better to offer the long option on the open market, catch the rest of the time premium alongside the option's inborn esteem, and utilize the returns toward buying the stock. At that point, you can convey the stock to the option holder at the higher strike cost.

Not Using Index Options in Neutral Trades

Singular stocks can be very unstable. For instance, if there is major unanticipated news in one specific organization, it may well shake the stock for a couple of days. Then again, even genuine turmoil in a noteworthy organization that is a piece of the S&P 500 presumably wouldn't make that list vary in particular.

Spread Trades

Most starting options traders attempt to leg into a spread by purchasing the option first and offering the second option at a later date. They're endeavoring to bring down the cost by a couple of pennies and it isn't justified regardless of the hazard.

Averaging Down

Most traders tend to wander across averaging down. It isn't what they had in mind when they first start to trade but end up doing so anyway. Several problems can arise when averaging down. The main thing is that they can lose a position that they are holding on to. This is sacrificing money and time. This money and time could be placed elsewhere that could prove itself to be better.

Struggling to Get Even

If you ever hope to be an expert trader, you need to get used to the idea of being wrong regularly and then work it into your business plan. Letting emotion come into play when you make the wrong bet will only lead you to make additional mistakes down the line. The goal should always be to focus on the cold logic behind the numbers, not a hunt for a way to improve your image or self-esteem. Always focus on price action, leave the worry about magic numbers, and breaking even for when trading is done for the day. The final win/loss ratio can't be tallied until the last trade is made.

Under or Overstaying Your Welcome

Many traders find that they have a good entry plan but a poor exit strategy. This, in turn, leads them to choose a less than ideal time to exit a given trade which leaves them stuck with an investment when they were only looking for a trade. If you find yourself in this scenario you must add detailed technical specifications that will determine when you will exit the trade in question. The specifics of this maneuver will likely change over time and it is common for the strategy to evolve over years, not weeks or months.

Gambling

While there is an inherent level of risk in every trade, there is a wide disparity between that and actual gambling. When trading your goal should always be to capitalize on predictive directional signals you have gleaned from checking the statistic, never to bet your money on a hunch. Your goal should be to ensure you remain as disciplined when it comes to making trades as possible. If you are interested in gambling with the stock market, you will likely find better odds for a return on investment in Las Vegas.

Mishandling Early Assignment

An early assignment occurs when a holder exercises an option that you are the writer upon much earlier than you had anticipated, and at terms that are much less favorable than you had initially hoped. If this happens, it can be easy to become flustered and simply sell as requested, taking a loss in the process. Instead, you must consider all the possible options, including purchasing another option for the express purpose of selling it, to ensure that you mitigate the extra costs as completely as possible.

Ignoring the Statistics behind Options Trading

One of the biggest mistakes that most newbie options traders make is that they forget that probability is a real thing. When you check a potential stock before purchasing an option, it's important to understand that the history of an option is important when deciding whether or not you should be investing in it, but so are the odds and probability surrounding whether or not a particular event will occur.

Being Overzealous

Oftentimes when new options traders finally get their initial plan just right, they become overzealous and start committing to larger trades than they can realistically afford to recover from if things go poorly. You must take it slow when it comes to building your rate of return and never bet more than you can afford to lose. Regardless of how promising a specific trade might seem, there is no risk/reward level at which it is worth considering a loss that will take you out of the game completely for an extended period. Trade reasonably and trade regularly and you will see greater results in the long term guaranteed.

Not Being Adaptable

Successful options traders know when to follow their plans, but they also know that no plan will be the right choice, even if early indicators say otherwise. There is a difference between making a point of sticking to a plan and following it blindly and knowing which is which one of the more important indicators of the separation is between options trading success and abject failure. This means you must be aware of when and where experimentation and new ideas are appropriate and when it is best to toe the line and gather more data to make a well-reasoned decision.

Ignoring the Probability

Always remember that the historical data will not apply to the current trends in the market at all times which means you will always want to consider the probability as well as the odds that the market behaves the way it typically does. The odds are how likely the market is to behave as expected and the probability is the ratio of the likelihood of a given outcome.

Not Dealing with Short Options Properly

While, in theory, it might seem like buying back short options at the last moment is the best choice, this practice is sure to hurt you more than helping you in the long run. It may be tempting to hold onto profitable options to squeeze the maximum return out of each investment, but you need to be aware that the potential for a reversal is always lurking in the shadows. Instead, a good rule of thumb is to buy back options that are currently at 80 percent of your ideal return or higher and let the extra take care of itself. While it may hurt to leave some potential profit on the table, it will improve your overall reliability, netting you a profit in the long run.

Not Considering Exotic Options

An exotic option is one that has a basic structure that differs from either European or American options when it comes to the how and when of how the payout will be provided or how the option relates to the underlying asset in question. Additionally, the number of potential underlying assets is much more varied and can include things like what the weather is like or how much rainfall a given area has experienced. Due to the customization options and the complexity of exotic options, they are only traded over the counter.

Buying Out of the Money Call Options

Most options traders adhere to the strategy of buying low and selling high. However, when you buy out of the money calls, you hurt your chances of making a profit, and when the losing streak becomes prolonged, it could render your trading strategy unproductive. Those highly susceptible to this mistake are the traders who operate on a small budget.

Giving in to Fear and Greed

Options trading requires a trader to be very forward-thinking and in charge of their emotions. But traders don't always exercise their emotional intelligence. For instance, when a trade is winning, an investor might get greedy and resist closing their position, simply because they want to allow the trade more time to go even further up. Greed can also manifest when an options trader is adamant although they are losing consistently. When losses become your constant companion, it's time to pull out and reevaluate your strategies. If you're executing appropriate trading strategies, there's no reason you should struggle to make a profit. Traders who are driven by fear tend to overreact to every small thing that goes wrong. For instance, they bail out at the first sign of incurring a loss.

Doing Poor Allocation

Never commit more than 5% of your portfolio to one options trade. As much as options have leverage and high earning potential, you cannot ignore the high level of risk exposure. Thus, you have to allocate prudently.

Having a Finite Approach

Options are flexible and can work with almost any securities market. But a single trading strategy doesn't achieve the same results across all securities markets. If an underlying asset is hardly moving, an out of the money call or put option is likely to expire worthlessly. However, taking covered options can be profitable in this scenario. Iron Condor, a trading strategy that involves taking many positions, would generate a profit if the underlying moves slowly.

Not Having an Exit Plan

Before you start trading, you should fully understand what you're trying to get into. How much money do you intend to make? What are your risk-reduction measures? Once you have answered the critical questions, you will be in a position to make appropriate strategies and learn how to exit with the least possible scars when you're losing money.

Ignoring Consistent Profits in Favor of Home Runs

Options traders tend to forgo the chance of making small yet consistent amounts of profits and focus their energies on nailing the elusive home run. If you have a trading strategy that seems to net you small but consistent earnings, you should stick to that.

Having a Strategy That Doesn't Match Your Outlook

An options trader is supposed to have an outlook of what they expect to happen. Technical analysis and fundamental analysis play a part in developing your outlook. Technical analysis promotes the interpretation of the market's volume and price on a chart, whereas fundamental analysis is mostly about reviewing a company's performance data. Thus, a trader must always take the trading strategy that marries their outlook.

Attempting to Recover Past Losses

A trade can move against you and make you lose money. Most traders have been there. Sometimes you may put your capital on options, and the outcome is not exactly what you expected. In such a scenario, most traders tend to double up their options strategy to see if they can recover the loss. Doubling may lower your potential for loss in a given trade, but it is surrounded by a lot of risks.

Trading in Illiquid Options

Liquidity in options trading refers to having active sellers and buyers on the market all the time. This is what drives competition. It also affects ask and bid prices for options and stocks. The stock market is often more liquid than the options market because stock traders focus on one commodity, while options traders often have several contracts to select from. An option quote always has the bid price and the asking price indicated on it. These prices do not indicate the actual value of the option. Illiquidity in options trading may result from illiquid stock. It is therefore important to trade options that are derived from a highly liquid stock.

Chapter 15: The Components of an Option Contract

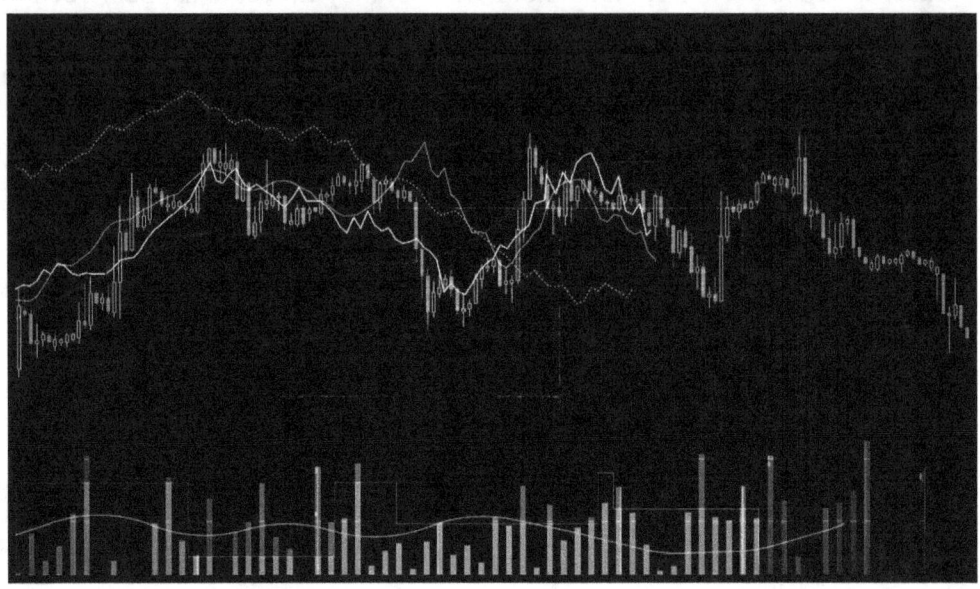

The Role of the Underlying Stock

It's vital to understand that stocks do play a fundamental role in options trading, even though they are not what you are buying and selling. Bear in mind that an option is only a piece of paper that gives you the right to buy or sell that stock–without the stock, you would have nothing to buy or sell.

You might say that the stock is Oz behind the curtain, changing and moving while your attention is fixed elsewhere. Letting Oz get up to his tricks without you is a bad idea–you need to be keeping an eye on your stocks just as much as you do the options themselves.

Not every stock is allowed its options to be traded on an options exchange. In total, you'll find somewhere in the region 3600 stocks spread across 12 different exchanges, though this number changes all the time.

What does this mean? Well, the exchanges have in place some very solid rules that dictate which stocks may and may not participate in options trading. You'll find some of the biggest business names on the planet there, and you'll also find what are known as "penny stocks," which buy and sell for less than $3.

In general, the latter won't do you much good for options trading. There simply isn't enough liquidity in such a small number for you to bother with the effort required to trade on them.

Instead, I would recommend sticking with the big names–the recognizable companies, such as Microsoft, Apple, Google, and McDonald's.

Another point to bear in mind is that there is a fixed relationship between options trading and its underlying stock. One option contract will always equal a hundred stock shares.

In other words, a single contract will give you the right to buy or sell 100 shares (or one stock). Multiply the number of contracts involved in a trade by 100 and you'll know how many shares are also involved.

The third factor of that relationship between an option and its underlying stock: whenever the stock goes up or down, in most cases, so too will the option contract.

Because the two are so inextricably linked, you will need to study the stock market in detail to be whizzing at options trading. You will need to be able to predict which stocks are going to head in which direction and when–only if you get this right will your trading be truly successful.

For that reason, a lot of options traders started with the stock market itself, giving themselves the experience of its whims before taking a step up to the next level. If you haven't done this, it will be worth spending a month or three tradings on the stock market, even a theoretical portfolio that you manage in a folder rather than on your own desktop and never pay a penny to invest in is a helpful step.

Doing this will allow you to get a sense of how the market functions overall and will familiarize you with some of the stocks you might be interested in trading on with options. The best options traders have almost a sixth sense of how an underlying stock is going to perform. The only way to develop that uncanny ability is through exposure, research, and experience.

Understanding the Strike Price

The strike price is the fixed price at which the underlying stock can be either sold or bought. When you purchase a call option, what you are purchasing is the right to buy that stock at this price, while selling a call option means that you are selling the right for your buyer to purchase the stock at that price.

The strike price is an aspect of every options trade that you will want to hone in on every time–it's that important. Never forget that, if the underlying stock never reaches that strike price, the trade is worthless because the option will simply expire on the deadline.

The difference between the current market price of the stock and the strike price of the option also represents the profit-per-share you can expect to make.

Let's say, for example, that you find two trades on a stock that is currently worth $150. One has a strike price of $125 and the other has a strike price of $100.

In the first trade, the stock price will need to drop to $125 before you have the right to buy or sell it (depending on whether the option is a call or a buy). In the second, it will need to drop to $100 before you get that right.

The value of the option is simple to calculate: it's the difference between the strike price and the current worth of the stock. In the first of these examples, the trade has a potential worth of $25; in the second, the potential worth is $50.

At first glance, it would seem to mean that the second option is the one to go for because its value is so much higher. However, you also need to bear in mind that you cannot dictate what the market does.

This is where the risk comes in. How confident are you, in this example, that the stock will plummet $50 before the expiration date of the option? If you're as certain as it's possible to be, it's a great investment. If you're not, you stand to lose the premium you paid for the option, because it will never reach the price at which you have the right to realize the trade.

The trade that has a strike price of $25 is, therefore, a sure bet–it's always going to be more likely that a stock will rise or fall by the smaller amount than the larger one. The trade-off, as you can see, is that you won't make nearly the profit you would on the riskier option, so you have to ask yourself whether the premium you'd be paying is worthwhile.

Strategy for Selling Covered Calls

We've covered the process, but what about the strategy behind it? We looked at the absolute basics of that strategy, but an experienced trader knows there's always going to be more to an option than meets the eye.

There's a whole list of considerations that you will eventually want to bear in mind as you expand your knowledge and develop your own personal strategy. Every trader has a different attitude towards what works and what doesn't—there are plenty of ways to make selling a covered call work, but you'll probably find yourself preferring one or two strategies.

We'll take a look now at those considerations in more detail to guide you as you delve into the covered call more deeply:

The Market Environment

You are no doubt aware that traders of stocks and shares are happy in a bull market and disgruntled in a bear market. You may also know that such traders hate a flat market most of all because very little is happening and there aren't many big profits to be made. For you, as a seller of covered calls, the opposite is true. I highly recommend waiting for the market to temporarily flatten before embarking on a spate of covered call sales. This is because you're only really interested in small changes to your share prices—if they are skyrocketing, you're losing more money on your contract. There also isn't as much danger of the bottom falling out of the market and your stock prices plummeting at the same time, which would be problematic.

Your Underlying Stock

There is nothing more important to your success than choosing the right stocks to invest in the first place. I cannot stress strongly enough that your success will be heightened if you pick stocks that move up very slowly. You don't want stocks that rise and fall very quickly, especially as a beginner, because they have a habit of making surprising moves that ruin your strategy. If they drop too far, you stand to lose a lot of money in the sale; if they rise too high, you lose the money you could have made if you'd sold them at that price. Traders who deal at risk often enjoy these stocks because they have higher premiums and a chance for huge profits, but that goes against the idea of selling covered calls: you're looking for a steady income that will underpin your riskier strategies elsewhere. By all means, go for the riskier stock elsewhere in your strategy, but avoid it like the plague for this particular function.

The Premium

Always remember that the premium is your guaranteed profit. Whatever else happens, you're going to walk away with that cash. When you factor in the cost to list the option and any commission you will lose to your broker, you'll be able to calculate the actual profit you'll make on that premium. Set yourself a minimum premium—a number that you consider to be enough to provide a profit you'll be happy with, on the assumption that it's the only profit you make. When you move ahead on setting the strike price, you'll likely adjust this base figure up or down based on what you think the underlying stock is going to do before the expiration date. Remember that the premium is only one component of the overall profit you will make—if you then set a strike price that means you lose the same amount of cash on selling the shares as you made through the premium, the trade wasn't worth doing in the first place.

The Expiration Date

There's a reason that the premiums on covered calls get higher the further out the expiration date. It's because, much like the weather forecasts we all deride daily, it gets harder and harder to predict what's going to happen to a share price the further out you go. Also bear in mind that your money is going to be tied up until the expiration date, so the premium will increase as a nod to that sacrifice. Most investors believe that a period between a month and three months works best.

The Strike Price

You might think that the strike price you set should be based on what you, as the seller, are comfortable with, but actually, it's the opposite. You're looking for a strike price that your buyer will feel comfortable with because otherwise, they aren't going to buy. That, in turn, is going to be dictated by the expiration date you set, as well as the premium you're asking for and how stable or volatile the underlying stock is. Your best bet is to put yourself in the shoes of your buyer: would you purchase that contract? How much would you stand to gain? Set your strike price accordingly and then take a look at it from your own point of view. Would this be an acceptable profit for you? If so, you've hit the nail on the head.

Chapter 16: How to Start Trading in Options

Would you agree that optional trading is exceptional? Some of you may not agree with this because you are fond of trading in the shares or the currencies which you consider less risky and volatile. How would you feel playing around with a figure which future-oriented? Like a game of chess where you fill a puzzle of uncertainties, it is the same deal with optional trading where you do not know the future. Most of you discredit this trading because you think it is filled with uncertainties. However, with useful speculation of the trade, it will not earn you much of the risk. There are certain things you as a beginner you ought to follow. The following strategies to come up with the right option.

First is that you have to think of your investment objective. You do not go there in the trading aimlessly because you will lose a lot of money. Remember that options require that intelligent speculation because you are dealing with future gains. You have to establish realistic and measurable values that you expect. Such goals will give you a way to go and the route to follow. You may plan which type of optional trading you want. That is where you want the put off option or the call option. Moreover, do you want to speculate on the performance of the underlying asset or hedge out their risks?

You have to examine the risks and the returns that the assets may bring you. Your biggest aim is always to harness sizeable gains while reducing the risks. You think that there are risks in the present and decide to buy them in the future. Or you with the put-up option you predict that the shares will fall in the price and you award others right for protecting their expected depreciation. You have to be tolerant, optimistic, and persistent in your tasks. If you are a risk-taker, this is the right avenue for you. If you sense a volatile market exploit that opportunity to gain much.

Identify the different events of the market of the sector you are trading. Those events will institute the volatility of the occurrence. You can either experience a drift or a rise in the market. Those events can be grouped in two ways, where one is the market-wide, and the other is the stock specif. The market-wide are like those government jurisdictions that affect the economy of the whole sector. For example, the government banning or subsidizing some products. In the stock-specific one, they include issues like product launches and many others.

You have to derive the right strategies after knowing the stocks to trade and the returns you desire. These are distinctive tactics that you will apply to harness many gains. You must be that intelligent speculator who will read the patterns and try to realize the peak points and the volatility of the market. Moreover, device some strategies like selling a call option against the stock. That is a tactic where you exercise a covered call approach on the security that you already own. You must sell the cover calls against your shares to identify the profitable spot. The other strategy is using the bullish or bearish strategy for the call option and the put option, respectively. Always buy puts options on significant stock platforms where you anticipate a substantial fallout of the top players in the industry.

Decide on the right parameter to facilitate your marketing. These are like the variables you will use to make a successful trading. Remember that for this trade, it requires one to know the trend, price analysis, and many other types.

Steps of Optional Trading for a Beginner

The first thing is to identify the right brokerage account. You can do that by researching those that pay well and with the right features. You can still seek recommendations from expert dealers. Check on their websites and create an account by keying in your correct details. Therefore, try to log in where you should remember your password vividly.

When you log in to that platform, you will be asked to select the right trade options you want. By now you should know the firm you want to buy from which you choose. It depends on the brokerage account because you should click on the odder or trade platform after identifying the shares to buy. This page should be clearly labeled, where click on to go to the next phase.

Search for the specific stock you want to buy. If you cannot find it in the list of the many securities, search for it in the search box. There will be multiple displays of the live quotes of shares that are being traded, hence select the one you want to buy. Still, you can navigate on the quote table to identify the primary and the options. Chose those alternatives because they are the reasons you are doing the trading.

Then there is the maturation month option where you must identify the peak times. That expiry period is the point where your contract ends; thus, you should set it according to your potential. The month should be realized when you have studied how the market behaves. You may have discovered that in a particular month the selling of shares is relatively high while in another period they are low. Choose that month that looks productive on your strike index.

Selecting your strike is the second last step. That is the amount of an asset in the predetermined period. It should level up to what you can afford and oversee if it generates good revenue. You should not set the illogical or unrealistic figure just because you want to earn more. Know your potential and the size of your wallet.

Select the put or call options that are found in different columns of the table. Usually, calls are grouped on the left and the puts on the right. Recognize the side you want to venture.

There is a platform for the quantity too. That is where you should fill the number of contracts you want to trade. Moreover, set the price to pay for the option. Check and recheck the orders, when everything is clear now is right for you to confirm and send.

Chapter 17: The Supports and Resistances

The chart patterns in any kind of trade calls for support and resistance. Whether you are dealing with fired trading, commodities, stocks, futures, or options. In any world of trading, it is the basis of the chart patterns. To understand better what support and resistance mean in the options trade, you can relate to the most common type of trade that is easily accessed by almost everyone because everyone is involved in at least one type of trade in the market.

Let's take an example of a situation where you go to the market to purchase a commodity that you've been using frequently. In this case, you are the bull. This is a product that you like so much and to encourage the seller to restock this product, there's that price that you will support so hard that you don't want it to fall. This is what we refer to as 'Support.' The buyer takes control of the prices and protects it so that it doesn't go down. The reason why the buyer would want to prevent the price from going down to the extreme is because of the fear that the seller would stop bringing the commodity on the market because they won't see its value. This is the concept of support that can be easily understood by anyone.

For resistance, it's the other way round. Here the seller now takes control of the price and prevents it from rising higher. For trading to carry on successfully, the buyer and the seller must agree on a specific price. Raising the price too high may make the bull reconsider an alternative commodity with a lower price depending on the amount of money they would want to spend. On the other hand, the seller would not consider trading at an extremely lower price than what they expect. This is because no one easily accepts a loss. Selling at weird spoils the motive that someone had for participating in the market.

Investors trade depending on the price levels. For instance, someone would prefer to purchase a good when the price of commodities is at a level where it is more likely to shoot after some time. When it happens as per their expectations, then it's a favor on their side because they are going to record again when they resell the commodity. This level where a large number of investors tend to believe that the prices will rise higher is what is known as the support level. It is what determines the decisions made by the majority of investors. When a support level is broken, it changes its worth and becomes the new resistance level.

At the resistance level, the investors always assume that the prices will fall lower. This makes the major investors think otherwise. Those who purchase commodities in bulk when the price is lower and is expected to move higher would not want to proceed to purchase the same commodity when they know that the price is more likely to drop so low that if they go ahead and sell it at that price, they will record a huge loss. Also, when the resistance level is broken, it changes and becomes the new support level.

On many occasions in the market, you will realize what is referred to as 'Noise'. This is when there are errors in pricing making them go beyond limits. The tops and bases of pricing are exceeded which may lead to misunderstanding between the bulls and the bears. However, this is a normal activity in the market and the traders always take care of it to ensure that trade moves on, even though it always brings some disagreements in most cases.

Beginner traders must always understand the concept of support and resistance to enable them to trade successfully without having diverted minds on what they are doing. When they get to understand how the market prices fluctuate with different seasons, they will be in a position to decide which commodity to trade with during what season. The errors associated with market pricing should be clearly understood by the beginner trades to prevent them from getting stranded when the price levels change from time to time.

Someone new to the trading market is sometimes made to believe that when the commodity prices are low, they are definitely meant to rise higher after some time, and this is where they normally get disappointed when the prices fall lower. Normally, the prices go extremely down, and this is always assumed to occur when new goods arrive in the market and replace the old ones.

Buyers and sellers must always agree upon the prices of every commodity. This is because the investors' plans are always different from the plans of any other normal trader. Understanding the level prices is not always easy for beginner traders but once they get used to it, trading becomes easy for them and they find it more comfortable dealing with different clients. Maintaining support levels and resistance levels helps both the bulls and bears to maintain a good trading relationship and remain positive about the results of the trade.

A good support level encourages the investors to invest more in the commodity with the belief that when they will be exchanging this particular commodity at a later date, the market prices will be fair on their side making them earn a reasonable profit. Everyone has a different preference when it comes to trading. Setting a higher resistance level can sometimes make it difficult for the seller to earn the expected profit. This normally happens when the buyers shift to a lower price commodity and let go of yours because it is not affordable to them. This only leads to you

Chapter 18: Risk and Reward

Risk is at the heart of all types of investment as without it there would be a need for reward. As such, options trading is risky at the best of times, even for those who might be considered experts and certainly for those who are still new to the field. Luckily, there are certainly ways to mitigate that risk as many of the major pitfalls of options trading have been well documented by those who have come before. What's more, they have also been distilled down and classified so that all you need to do is memorize the following and ensure that you do your best not to let it intrude on your trading success.

It doesn't matter what type of trade you are working with, the first thing you are going to want to do is to consider three main things. First, you will want to be aware of how much a specific price is likely going to change before the expiration of the option in question. From there, you will want to determine how volatile the underlying asset is as well as how much time the option has to turn you a profit before its expiration. When you are purchasing options, it is important also to identify the direction you expect the underlying stock to move in as well as how long you expect it to continue to move in the specified direction. In these instances, the amount of time that is still available won't be as important when it comes to ensuring the overall maximum value.

To ensure that you minimize risk, it is important to keep in mind that the best strategies are those that focus on either high positive risk value or high negative risk value; there is little value in betting on the middle ground. Remember, some option types are always going to end up being more profitable than others in specific scenarios, you just need to have the patience and the foresight to know what's coming before it gets here. With that being said, however, it is important to always keep in mind that statistical projections cannot actually tell the future which means that any analysis that is done is strictly hypothetical. Never invest more money into a particular trade, no matter how reliable it seems, than you can ultimately afford to lose.

When it comes to making trades in groups, or combining them in other ways, it is important to consider the net risk of the entire trade instead of focusing on the specific risk likelihoods of parts of the whole. This will make it easier for you to determine the most profitable way to move forward at any juncture because it makes the risk/reward split much easier to analyze.

Remember, there are multiple different types of risk which means that understanding what each means for your specific trade is crucial to covering all your bases and making successful options trades on a reliable basis.

Delta

Delta can be thought of as the amount of overall risk that you take on depending on how likely the underlying asset in question is going to move before the point where the option expires. If the asset is at the money at the moment, then the delta is going to be .5. What you can take from this is the fact that when the underlying asset moves a single point in either direction then the option will move .5 points. Puts are always going to have a delta of somewhere between -1 and 0 and calls will always have a delta that is somewhere between 1 and 0.

Delta should always be the first type of risk that you consider as it will do the most to help you immediately determine if a specific trade is going to be in your best interest or not. You will find that it is the most helpful when it can be used to make decisions related to puts you are interested in making as it will help make it clear the direction the underlying asset is going to be likely to move in. To determine the delta, you are going to want to start by considering historical data related to the underlying assets by looking at previous strike prices in comparison to their comparable puts. When it comes to measuring delta, it is important to keep in mind that cheaper options are naturally going to have a lower delta. This occurs naturally as delta measures the chance an option will be profitable at expiration. This is why you are going always to want to avoid options with a delta that is either .4 or -.4 because it is rather unlikely that they are going to end up being favorable trades by the time everything is said and done.

Rho

Rho is the name given to the quantity of risk that surrounds the interest rates relating to an underlying asset and the probable that changes in this area will result in changes to the underlying asset price and thus negatively affect the price of the option as well. As a general rule, you can expect interest rates to increase along with call prices, causing a decrease in put values. The reverse of this statement will also be true, causing an increase in put prices and a decrease in interest rates. Rho is going to be the most influential when the price of the underlying asset is greater than or equal to the option price. Calls will always have a positive Rho and puts will always have a negative rho. Rho is going to be relevant primarily to those who are interested in options trading as a form of long-term investment.

Gamma

If delta measures the amount of change that occurs between the underlying asset and the option in question, then gamma measures the likelihood that the delta is going to remain the same as long as the option remains active. The larger the gamma grows, the closer the underlying asset and the related option are likely to be to one another and a smaller gamma means that the variation between them is quite large because the stock has fallen beneath the strike point. Big gammas mean big profits but also larger degrees of risk. Additionally, you will want to keep in mind that the gamma will increase naturally as it gets closer to the point at which the option is going to expire. If you need to know just how much the gamma is likely to increase during this period you can certainly find out, all you need to do is consider the gamma of the gamma.

Theta

Theta is a representation of the rate at which the time the option has left is currently expiring in comparted to how much time it has as a whole. Theta starts as a positive amount that starts to tick down the instant that an option comes into existence. Theta decreases at a steady rate compared to the price of the related option as it is guaranteed to lose value each second it ticks closer to expiration. A trade will remain profitable for the holder as long as the delta remains greater than theta and will make money for the writer once this balance reverses itself.

As an options trader, it is important always to be aware of the fact that theta will constantly be changing, and that this change will increase in frequency the closer the option it is measuring gets to its expiration point. Theta is going to be the most important variable to consider if you are planning to make a trade based on the assumption that the market is not going to change before the options expiration. If this is not the case, then theta will be the least relevant element of risk to your trades as long as you work around it as needed.

Vega

Vega is the type of risk that measures how volatile the underlying asset is compared to the market as a whole. Vega can be difficult to accurately determine at points, simply because it is possible to change although the price of the asset it points to remain neutral during the same period. As such, making a successful options trade doesn't mean being able to avoid Vega completely, it means understanding how to take advantage of it regardless of the level of volatility that is in play.

Different options are going to respond in different ways to increasing Vega; those that respond positively are known as long volatility options and those that respond negatively are called short volatility options. Options that have long volatility will have a positive amount of Vega and short volatility options are going to have a mega Vega. If you find an option with a neutral Vega, then it will have a neutral level of volatility to go along with it.

Chapter 19: Basic Options Strategies Going Long

While it can be easy to feel as though there is too much information out there regarding options trading to ever hope to keep it straight, there are several key strategies you will regularly use that you can focus on at the start to make the entire process far more manageable. As long as you take the time to utilize them correctly, you will find that each of the strategies outlined below will dramatically improve your success rate while decreasing your overall risk at the same time.

Keep in mind that the strategies that you use aren't nearly as important as the fact that you choose strategies that suit your trading style and compliments the trading plan you are focused on using for the time being. Keep in mind that just because a strategy seems useful, doesn't mean it is going to be useful in your hands.

Play name: Married Put

Details: A married put is a great strategy if you have reason to take a bullish attitude towards the price of a given underlying asset while at the same time aiming to shore up any potential losses you might come across. To use this strategy properly, the first thing you will need to do is to purchase any amount of the underlying asset in question while at the same time purchasing a put that covers the same amount. This will act as the price floor that will help you to prevent serious, unexpected losses in the case of a sudden price drop.

While the married put will not be the best choice in any situation, if used in the right way, and with plenty of caution, it can be a reliable way to improve your successful trading percentage successfully. To ensure this always works out in your favor, you will never want to begin a new transaction without having a clear understanding of the risk you are working with beforehand. You will then be able to factor in additional costs more easily and compare the total cost to the amount of risk you are going to mitigate as a result.

After that, all that's left is going to be doing the math and choosing the option that makes the most fiscal sense at the moment. What's more, married puts also help to reduce the risk potential when it comes to early options to exercise as it ensures you always have available shares waiting in the wings.

Play name: Bull Call Spread

Details: To utilize the bull call spread successfully, you will want to start with a call option that is purchased at a strike price that is worth returning to in the future. You will also need to sell an equal number of calls at a strike price that is above the initial strike price yet still within a reasonable distance. Both of these calls will also need to include the same timeframe as well as the same underlying asset. This is an excellent strategy to use if you feel bullish on the strength of the asset in question or you have research that shows the price is likely to increase during your chosen timeframe.

This strategy also goes by the name vertical credit spread thanks to its mismatched legs. Those that sell close to the money result in a credit spread that includes a positive time value and a net credit. Debit spreads are created if a short option ends further away from the money than the point it started from. Regardless, you can consider this strategy a net buy.

Play name: Bear Put Spread

Details: Similar in practice to the bull call spread, the bear put spread is useful under opposite circumstances. To use it effectively, you will need to purchase a pair of put options that have different strike prices, own lower and one higher. You will then need to purchase an equal number with the same timeframe and the same underlying asset. This can be an especially useful strategy if you have a bearish opinion of the underlying asset in question as it will help to limit your losses if you judge the market incorrectly. It is still important to be cautious; however, as the profits that it will bring, you are always going to be limited to the difference between the two puts you initially purchased, minus any relevant fees.

The most profitable time to utilize this strategy is if you are already planning on short selling a specific underlying asset and a traditional put option won't provide you with the protection you need. You will likely find them especially useful if you plan on speculating and also feel that prices are going to decrease. This will allow you to avoid employing additional capital while only waiting for the worst to happen. As such, you will be able to hope for the best and plan for the worst at the same time.

Details: The protective collar strategy can be executed by buying into a put option that is already out of the money. From there, you will then want to write a secondary call option that is based on the same underlying asset and is also out of the money. After that, you will then be able to create one already. Thus, this strategy is useful if you are already committed to a long position on an underlying asset that has a history of strong gains. Using a protective collar properly then allows you to ensure that you can anticipate a steady level of profit while also retaining control of the underlying asset if the positive trend does continue.

Play name: Straddle

Details: The straddle can be used to either go long or short. The long straddle can be extremely effective if you feel as though the price of a given underlying asset is going to move significantly in one direction, you just don't know what direction that will ultimately be. To utilize this strategy, you will need to purchase a put and a call, both using the same underlying asset, strike price, and timeframe, after the long straddle has been created successfully you will be guaranteed to generate a profit if the price in question moves in either direction before it expires.

Play name: Strangle

Details: Functionally, strangle is similar to a straddle except that it is often cheaper to execute on as you are buying into options that are already out of the money. As such, you can typically pay as much as 50 percent of the cost of a straddle for strangling which makes it even easier to play both sides of the fence. Typically, a long strangle is more useful than a short straddle because it offers up twice the premium for the same amount of risk.

To use the long strangle correctly, you will want to purchase a call along with a put that is both based on the same underlying asset with the same timeframe and different strike prices. The strike price for the call will need to be above the strike price for the put and both should be out of the money. This strategy can be especially useful if you plan on the underlying asset moving a great deal without having a clear idea as to the direction. When used properly, this will virtually ensure you turn a profit once you have taken any fees out of the equation.

Play name: Butterfly Spread

Details: A butterfly spread is a combination of a bear spread and a traditional bull strategy that uses a total of three strike points. To begin with, you will need to purchase a call option at the lowest point you can manage before selling a pair of calls at a higher price and then a third call that has an ever-higher price. Your end goal with these purchases is to make sure that you have a range of prices you can profit from when everything is said and done.

This strategy can prove particularly effective when you have a completely neutral opinion on the current market. What's more, you should also expect the underlying asset to move in the direction you favor, even if you don't have all the details locked down just yet. This then means that you will want to strive to keep the market volatility as low as possible. The greater the overall level of volatility, the greater the cost of this strategy will be. Furthermore, it is extremely important to keep in mind that if you choose incorrectly when it comes to the direction the underlying asset is going to move, then the amount you stand to lose can be significant.

Play name: Iron Condor

Details: To utilize the iron condor strategy, you will need to begin by taking a short position as well as a long position via a pair of strangles that is situated so they will take full advantage of a market that is staunchly low volatility. The pair of strangles should include both a long and a short, with both sets to the outer strike price. You can accomplish the same general effect with a pair of credit spreads if you are so inclined. In this scenario, the call spread would be placed above the market price and the put would be placed beneath the current market price.

Play name: Iron Butterfly

Details: The iron butterfly strategy can be anchored by either a short straddle or a long straddle, depending on your needs. Regardless, you will want to then orchestrate strangle based on the straddle you needed to use. The iron butterfly utilizes a mixture of puts and calls to limit the potential for loss (but also profits) around the strike price you formerly determined. This strategy is best used with options that are out of the money as they allow you to minimize both risk and cost.

ROI or Return on Investment

The Term ROI stands for Return on Investment. ROI is a measure of performance and is used by both investors and traders to measure the effectiveness and efficiency of an investment. This includes your trading capital. ROI deliberately endeavors to measure directly the total return derived from a particular investment.

One of the most important aspects of your investment portfolio is its profitability. You need to regularly monitor your investments, which are best achieved using the ROI or return on investment. It is advisable to work out what each dollar invested has generated. There is a formula for working out this figure.

R.O.I = (Profits - Costs) / Costs

Even then, investors need to understand that the ROI depends on numerous other factors such as the kind of investment security preferred and so on. Also, note that a high ROI implies a higher risk, while a lower figure means reduced risk. For this reason, appropriate risk management must be undertaken.

A Brief Introduction to Technical Analysis

What is technical analysis? It is simply a method used by traders, investors, and other market players to examine and predict price movements in the markets. Technical analysis makes use of market statistics as well as historic chart prices. The idea behind this type of analysis is that identifying past market performance can help to accurately predict future performance.

As a trader, you want to be able to identify the shares to trade, the best entry points, volumes, price, and the best exit points. The best way to find out information about all these is through technical analysis.

Two Different Approaches

According to finance experts, there are two basic approaches to technical analysis. These are the top-down approach and the bottom-up approach. In most cases, short-term traders will opt for the top-down approach, while long-term investors prefer the bottom-up approach.

Chapter 20: Choosing a Broker

Brokers and Trading Platforms

The use of shares, whether it is to collect dividends or to speculate on their listing, is an increasingly widespread and interesting practice. The risk of loss is always present but depending on the way you buy and sell your shares; this risk can be reduced. If you are wondering how to buy and sell the shares of large, listed companies online, here are some explanations that may interest you.

Buy shares to become shareholders

A large part of private individuals and institutions that buy stocks do so to become shareholders.

It is the simplest use of actions and their main purpose.

In fact, when a company issues its shares, it is possible to buy them directly online.

However, for the already listed shares to do so, it is necessary to go through an intermediary, which can be an online broker or an online bank.

Buy and Sell Shares with Online Banks

The easiest way to buy and sell shares is to go through one of the placement products offered by banks and, in particular, by online banks. Thanks to the 100% online operation of these banks, you can easily pass your purchase and sale orders directly via the internet without moving.

The advantages of this system are numerous because it is your bank that will take care of executing your orders and then buying and selling your shares. To take advantage of stock market shares through these systems, you must underwrite an Investment Plan in Shares, a securities account, or life insurance, which are the main banking products on the stock market. The only drawback of this method concerns the expenses that may be higher than those that you would have to pay if you bought and sold the shares yourself.

However, bank commissions rarely exceed 4%.

One of the main advantages of bank placement products is that market intermediaries supervise your purchases and sales of shares and you can benefit from advice.

Buy and sell shares with online brokers

Another method is to contact an online mediator. Their operation is almost identical to that of online banks, with the difference that you do not enjoy assistance and advice, but at the same time, the costs are lower because you decide for yourself what actions to buy or sell.

These online brokers also allow trading through stock market shares, without actually having to buy them. To do this, you just need to speculate on the evolution of their value. The tools that allow you to proceed in this way are CFDs.

Ultimately there are several methods to buy and sell shares on the internet. Before deciding on one or other of these solutions, take care to correctly evaluate the commissions involved as well as your level of knowledge on the stock exchange. Depending on these criteria, each of these two methods has different advantages. It is also good to understand the quotation system of an action to be able to speculate on this type of asset.

Choosing and using a financially sound and responsive brokerage should be a high priority for every trader. And that brokerage should provide access to every trading venue: equities, options, futures, or forex. Many brokerages are running slick TV ads that do not qualify. When you examine the list of financial products served by brokerages, you may be disappointed. Some well-known brokerages support stocks and options. But they do not offer futures or foreign exchange. So, walk away and keep looking.

Many who are new to trading select a brokerage because they know someone who has an account with that particular brokerage. But this is not how you should choose your brokerage, particularly if you are an entry-level trader. Conduct some research before you make a final decision. You want to choose a brokerage that fits your investment and trading style. This may not be the same as your friend's.

Fortunately, you can use the Internet to evaluate brokerages. A website provided by the Financial Industry Regulatory Authority (FINRA) provides a substantial amount of information about the conduct of both individuals and firms. Of course, it essentially lists regulatory citations, and never makes recommendations or posts complimentary comments. The listed regulatory citations are mostly for failures in oversight or careless trading practices. Corresponding fines are also listed. You can read these to find FINRA citations similar to the following:

This permits you to see a list of former employers, the time a counselor has been working with financial securities, and any past FINRA citations that may exist.

Charts like these never tell the entire story. And like so much Internet content, they are often misleading. The range of securities supported in addition to the sophistication of the trading platforms was ignored. The Kiplinger rankings are far from accurate when you consider the breadth of services, platform technologies, number of branch offices, availability and quality of customer support, and more.

In the author's opinion, TD Ameritrade's thinkorswim platform would rank #1 for trading options and stocks. It has the most extensive feature set. And Trade Station, which is superior to many of those listed, wasn't even included. Furthermore, a trade that costs $0.0050/share looks good at first glance. But a 4,000-share trade costs $20 in commissions. Most experienced investors know brokerages will likely reduce their commissions and exchange fees to meet competition. This is especially true for high-net-worth clients and/or high-volume active traders.

Full-Service and Discount Brokers

Full-service brokers typically provide financial investment counselors. The counselors may suggest financial securities products, managed funds, or recommend investment management companies with which they maintain business relationships. These full-service brokerages also provide research and education to their clients. The fees charged by full-service brokers are usually higher than those charged by discount brokers. Required minimum account deposits may also be higher than those required at discount brokerages. Besides, the maintenance of a minimum account balance may be required.

Discount brokerages also require a minimum account deposit and the maintenance of a minimum account balance. This can range from $500 to $1,000. And experienced active traders who manage their own trading activity have little interest in receiving trading advice from an investment counselor, who may not have as much trading experience or knowledge as their clients.

Many old-timers have clear recollections of their dealings with the traditional brick and mortar brokerage houses and the so-called "stockbrokers" in their employ. They'd look at the lists of stocks in the daily news or the Wall Street Journal. When they spotted a trade opportunity, they'd phone their broker to put on a trade, and pay a $70 commission. They also remember receiving phone calls from their broker who had been advised by the "boys in New York" to solicit their clients to buy shares of stock that were part of an issue that their brokerage house was promoting. Some clients wised up and referred to these stocks as the "stock de jour."

This was an unscrupulous "pump and dump" practice used by brokerages to increase the sales of an underlying stock held within the brokerage's own portfolio. Once the solicitations drove the price up as a result of the sudden influx of buy orders, the brokerage dumped the stock for a profit, leaving their clients "holding the bag." Obviously, they couldn't do this every day, and it didn't take long for regulatory agencies and clients alike to catch on. But according to many, this actually happened. Today, the regulatory agencies watch for these kinds of practices and levy heavy fines when detected.

But stories like these often drive traders to the discount brokerages. All an experienced trader wants or needs for that matter is access to the market through a full-featured, reliable trading platform, reasonable commissions and exchange fees, and fast execution times.

Develop a checklist that evaluates prospective brokerages. Look for the following, arranged in no particular order:

- Account types (Brokerage, IRA Rollovers, checking, bill pay, savings, money market, etc.)
- Minimum balance requirement.
- Transaction fees.
- Margin interest rate.
- Supported trading venues (equities, options, futures, and/or forex)
- Execution speed.

- Access to different trading venues.
- Trading platforms (online for PCs and/or Macintosh Computers)
- Trade scanning engine(s).
- Market research (either web-based or trading platform-based)
- Account access via brokerage website.
- Trading via brokerage website.
- Earnings and dividend releases.
- Mobile trading apps (iPhone, Android, iPad, Android Tablets, Windows Mobile)
- Paper (simulated) trading for practice.
- Back trades (testing strategies with historical pricing data)
- Support (online chat, telephone, e-mail, and text messaging)
- Training (live and/or online)
- Complete financial reporting (monthly, year-to-date, prior years, 1099s, IRA minimum required distribution calculations, commissions paid, margin fees, etc.)
- Nearby branch offices.

Financial Security and Stability

When opening an account, you may want to know who is underwriting the security of your account in addition to the maximum amount protected. Congressional action in 1970 requires all brokerages to register with the Securities Investor Protection Corporation (SIPC). The SIPC is to brokerages what the FDIC is to banks. The SIPC protects the brokerage accounts of each customer. If the brokerage firm is closed due to bankruptcy or fraud, the SIPC protects customer assets up to $500,000 in securities and $100,000 in cash. If your accounts exceed these insured values, you may want to consider distributing your funds across more than one brokerage, although very few investors actually do this.

Although the SIPC protects against bankruptcy and fraud, it doesn't protect against market losses caused by a decline in security values. If a brokerage firm does fail, the SIPC works to merge the failed brokerage into a successful one. Failing this, the SIPC will transfer a client's securities to another firm. If stocks or bonds are missing from an investor's portfolio, the SIPC will rebuild portfolios by replacing every missing share of stock or bond, penny for penny, up to the insured limits.

Many investors never consider what can happen to their account holdings in the event of a run on the financial markets or an institution. What effect can this have on the stability of your broker, also called broker-dealer?

It's somewhat reassuring to know that during such condition's insurance is extended and liquidity facilities are created to back depositor accounts. The Securities and Exchange Commission (SEC) has instituted several reforms on liquidity. These liquidity reforms ensure that each broker-dealer maintains a suitable reserve to cope with inordinate levels of client withdrawals.

Despite these regulations, short-term unstable funding can prevent broker-dealers from order fulfillment. This can be due to a short-term lack of funds required to carry temporary imbalances in the volume of buy and sell orders. This impairs the ability of traders to buy and sell a wide variety of stocks and bonds. It can also have the effect of bringing trading to an abrupt halt.

Many investor-traders remember the failures of broker-dealers Lehman Brothers and Bear-Sterns during the housing mortgage fiasco of 2008. As a result of the lessons learned then, many broker-dealers have increased their capital holdings, increased liquidity, and reduced their holdings in risky assets. All of these policies are attempts to protect themselves against the reoccurrence of events like those that brought down these huge brokerage houses.

As the holder of a brokerage account, you should know that the potential for broker-dealer failures still exists. Both broker-dealers and banks have been encouraged to form either asset-rich bank holding companies or intermediate holding companies to help spread capital risk.

Broker-dealers typically find short-term security by negotiating repurchase agreements with underwriters, such as money market funds. This provides the financing needed by broker-dealers to fund their transactions. In exchange, the underwriters receive reasonably low financing fees. The money market funds, among a few others, avoid long-term, risky securities. They happily settle for shorter-term, low-risk securities with less vulnerability to a potential market run.

Chapter 21: Strangles and Straddles

Options allow you to create strategies that simply are not possible when investing in stocks. There are two ways that you can do this, they are known as strangles and straddles. This is a more complex strategy than simply buying a long call option or a long put. But it's not really that complicated, you just have to understand some basics on how to set them up to make a profit.

The strategy that is used in this case is dependent on a large move by the stock. There are many situations where this might be appropriate. But mainly, this is something you will consider using when you are looking to profit from an earnings call.

Earnings calls cause major price shifts in the big stocks. The price shift is largely determined by what the analyst's "expectations" are for earnings, and so this is not always a rational process. If the company beats the analyst expectations when it comes to earnings per share, this creates a positive "surprise" that will usually send the stock soaring. The amount of "surprise" is given by the percentage difference between the actual value and the expected value. So, in this case, if you had bought a call option, you could make amazing levels of profit from the option by selling it in the next day or two, as long as the new higher price level is maintained.

But the problem is, you have no idea beforehand whether the earnings are going to exceed or fail to meet the analyst expectations. The silly thing about this (from a common-sense perspective) is that even if the company is profitable if they fail to meet analyst expectations, these results in massive disappointment. So, you might see share prices drop from a sell-off even if the company is profitable. This is "surprise" in a negative way.

The impact of failing to meet expectations can be magnified if the company also has some bad news to share. This news hit Netflix stock hard, it dropped by a walloping $42. If you had purchased a put option, that could have meant a $4000 profit.

The problem is that you don't know ahead of time which way the stock is going to go. It's one thing to look back and say well you could have had a put option and made $4k in a day, but often companies reveal information in earnings calls that have been under wraps. Nobody had any inkling that Netflix was going to be losing subscribers until the earnings call.

Second, analyst expectations are somewhat arbitrary. Defining success or failure in terms of them is actually pretty silly, but that is the way things work right now. But the point is it's really impossible to know whether or not these arbitrary expectations are met before the earnings call. It's also impossible to gauge the level of reaction that is going to be seen from exceeding or failing to meet expectations.

Since we don't know which way the stock is going to move, it would seem that a good strategy to use is to buy a call and a put at the same time. That is precisely the idea behind a straddle and strangle.

That way, you profit no matter what happens, as long as the price on the market changes fairly strongly in one direction or another. When you set up a straddle or strangle, there is a middle "red zone" that bounds the current share price over which you are going to lose money. But if the share price either goes above the boundaries of this zone or below it, you will make profits.

If the stock shoots upward, this means that the put option is going to drop massively in value. So, it's basically a write off for you. But if the stock makes a strong move, as they often do after positive earnings calls, you stand to make enough profits from the call option that was a part of your trade to more than make up for the loss of the put. The potential upside gain is in theory unlimited. Of course, in practice, share prices don't rise without limit, but they might rise, $10, $20, or $40, and that could potentially earn profits of roughly $1,000-$4,000, more than covering any loss from the now worthless put option.

The opposite situation applies as well. If the stock drops by a large amount, you make profits. Profits to the downside are capped because a stock price cannot decline below zero. That said, if the stock drops by a significant amount, you can still make hundreds to thousands of dollars per contract virtually overnight.

Doing this requires some attention on your part. You are going to have to think ahead to implement this strategy and profit from it. Remember that you can use a straddle or strangle any time that you think the stock is going to make a major shift one way or the other. An example of a non-earning season situation, where this could be a useful strategy, would be a new product announcement. Think Apple. If Apple is having one of their big presentations, if the new phone that comes out disappoints the analysts, share prices are probably going to drop by a large amount. On the other hand, if it ends up surprising viewers with a lot of new features that make it the must-have phone again, this will send Apple stock soaring.

The problem here is you really don't know which way it's going to go. There are going to be leaks and rumors but basing your trading decisions on that is probably not a good approach, often, the rumors are wrong. A strangle or straddle allows you to avoid that kind of situation and make money either way.

Other situations that could make this useful include changes in management or any political interaction. We mentioned the government recently made a privacy settlement with Facebook. If you knew when the settlement was going to occur but wasn't sure what it was going to be, using strangle or straddle might be a good way to earn money from the large price moves that were sure to follow.

The same events that might warrant buying a long call such as a GDP number or jobs report, for options on index funds, are also appropriate for strangles and straddles.

Implied Volatility Strategy

Implied volatility is very important when a big event like an earnings report is coming. This gives you a way to make profits. In fact, we are going to call this the implied volatility strategy.

Remember, implied volatility is a projection of what the volatility of the stock is going to be in the near future. When there is an earnings call, the volatility is going to be extreme on the day after the call. Therefore, you are going to see the implied volatility growing as earnings day approaches.

At the time I am writing this, it is 24 hours before Facebook's earnings call. The implied volatility is 74%, which is very high. In contrast, for Apple, which is more than a week away from its next earnings call, the implied volatility is only 34%. This is for a $207.50 strike put, with a share price of $207.9.

The strategy is to profit from the implied volatility. You want to enter your position one to two weeks before the earnings call or big announcement. As implied volatility increases, this is going to swamp out time decay and cause a big rise in the option price.

Using that Apple put option if we assumed that there were only 4 days to expiration, but the implied volatility had risen to about where Facebook is and there were no other changes (so we will leave the share price where it was), the price of the put option would increase by about $330.

So if nothing else, you could profit from the change of implied volatility. It will probably go highest the day before the earnings call.

This is going to be magnified if you trade a strangle or straddle. Before the earnings call, both the put and the call option are going to increase a great deal in value because of implied volatility. So you could sell the strangle the day before the earnings call and book some profits then. Since a strangle or straddle can earn big profits if there is a large move in the share price, you won't find any problems locating a buyer.

Estimating Price from Implied Volatility

If you know the implied volatility, you can estimate the price range of the stock. This can be done using a simple formula.

(Stock price x implied volatility)/SQRT (days in a year)

If you don't want to do the calculation, if we take the square root of 365, it is about 19.1. For example, we use Facebook with a share price of $202.50 and an implied volatility of 76%.

Facebook	
Stock Price	$202.50
Implied Vol.	0.76
Days in a year	19.1049732
Expected Change	$8.06
Upper Range	$210.56
Lower Range	$194.44

The implied volatility gives us an idea of what traders are thinking, about the upcoming earnings call, but of course, we can never be sure what is really going to happen until it does. But this gives us upper and lower bounds. Using the information that we have available, we can guess that Facebook might rise to $210.56 a share after the earnings call, or it might drop to $194.44 per share after the earnings call. You can use these boundaries to set up your strategy. However, remember that if there is a big surprise, it can go well past these boundary points in one direction or the other.

What is a Long Straddle?

To set up a straddle, you buy a put option and a call option simultaneously (buy = take a long position). The maximum loss that you can incur is the sum of the cost to buy the call option plus the sum of the cost to buy the put option. This loss is incurred when you enter the trade.

With a straddle, you buy a call option and a put option together. And they would be with the same strike price. By necessity, this means that one option is going to be in the money and one option is going to be out of the money. When approaching an earnings call, the prices can be kind of steep, because you want to price them close to the current share price. That way, it gives us some room to profit either way the stock price moves.

A maximum loss is only incurred if you hold the position to expiration. You can always choose to sell it early if it looks like it's not going to work out and take a loss that is less than the maximum.

Chapter 22: How to Profit from Trading Options

Making money from trading options is rather straightforward. However, it largely depends on your understanding of the market. Thus, it is paramount that you get the proper know-how. As you gain more knowledge and experience, you'll be able to make more and more consistent profits.

Now, it's important to note that options naturally lose value over time. This is called "time decay." Therefore, time decay is proportionally inverse to the expiration of the contract. So, options contracts are more valuable the more time have before they expire. The reasoning behind this is that a contract that is very close to expiration does not provide the holder enough time to maneuver. In contrast, a contract that has plenty of time left on it can provide the holder with room to maneuver.

Let's look at an example.

A put option is valued at $100. This option is for 100 shares of a corporation valued at $1 apiece. Please keep in mind that the standard for options contracts is 100-share lots. So, if you wanted to purchase 500 shares, you could take out five 100-share contracts. Since the stock in question is highly coveted, the writer agrees to the deal while charging a premium of $0.10 per share. Thus, the total premium paid would be $10. Additionally, the contract is a one-month expiration.

On day one, the contract is worth $10, that is, the full premium that was paid for it. So, if you wanted to turn around and sell your rights, you could easily collect the $10. But if you decided to sell your rights on day 15, the contract would be worth roughly half of what you paid for it.

How so?

The contract only has half of its term left on it. So, it makes sense for a third party to pay only half of the premium. Now, suppose you tried to sell on day 27 or 28, you could reasonably expect to collect only a fraction of the original premium's value.

This is where savvy options traders can make money.

Savvy options traders like to scour the market to find contracts that are close to expiration. Then, they bid for the rights of the contract at a fraction of the original cost. The angle here is to pick up a cheap contract that provides an opportunity to pick up stock at a price point that's better than its current market valuation.

In the case of a call option, investors might be looking to buy shares at a lower price. However, there are none to be found. So, scouring the market for cheap options are a good alternative. If the opportunity is present, then a deal can be made.

Conversely, an investor might be looking to sell their shares. However, the current market valuation does not seem appealing. Hence, a put option makes sense. The investor purchases the rights to a contract at a reduced price and then sells the stock.

Consequently, time decay opens up the door for options traders to make money in two ways. Let's take the time now to explore these alternatives.

Buy Low, Sell High

In this strategy, investors use options to find shares at the desired price point. This means either taking out the option themselves or finding other parties willing to sell their rights. In either case, investors are looking to pick stocks at a much more favorable price.

Investors approach this strategy in one of two ways. Firstly, they go searching for open contracts on a specific stock. For example, investors search for open contracts on Apple or Microsoft stock. If they find them at their desired price point, they'll scoop them up. Secondly, investors search for open contracts in hopes of finding a good deal. Here, the company itself is not the target. Instead, the target is the contract itself. The company then becomes a secondary target. Naturally, if the company is not worth the risk, then it makes sense to pass on the contract.

So, let's explore how investors stand to profit under this approach.

Scenario #1:

An investor is interested in purchasing stock in a company. This company's current share price sits at $12.50 per share. As such, the investor looks for options to find a lower price point for the stock. The investor finds an open contract for the stock at $12 per share. The contract has a premium of $5 with 10 days remaining on a 30-day expiration. The investor purchases the rights to the contract for $2. Then, executes the contract. The investor gets the shares at $12 apiece. Then, they turn around and sell the stock at the current market valuation. They profit $0.50 per share minus the cost of the premium.

Scenario #2:

An investor is bargain hunting. They find an option that's about to expire. This is a call on a corporation that is currently valued at $13 a share. The option has a strike price of $12.75. The contract was two days left on its duration. So, the investor scoops up the contract for a fraction of its original value. Since the stock is currently valued above the strike price, the investor sees the potential for a quick profit. So, they scoop up the call paying a modest premium. Then, they immediately exercise the option. Once they have bought the stock at $12.75, they promptly sell at $13. The profit is $0.25 per share minus the premium.

In both of these scenarios, the investor needs to move quickly. The investor is keen on time. They know that acting quickly will maximize gains. Unlike the traditional "buy and hold" strategy, the "buy low, sell high" strategy requires investors to act fact. Otherwise, market shifts may zap their profits altogether. As such, the investor needs to take advantage of an expiring option while also cashing in on the current market valuation.

Using Options for Speculative Purposes

In the stock market, speculation is like gambling. Investors make bets on what they hope will or will not happen. In such cases, investors can use options contracts to place their bets. Options provide investors with the opportunity to make risky deals without exposing themselves to unwanted consequences.

Speculation consists of what you, as an investor, believe will happen even when you are not sure, if or when it will actually take place. When speculators hit a home run, they clean up. When they strike out, they can be wiped out.

Let's consider an example.

A corporation's stock is currently trading at $16 a share. Historically, this company's stock has traded between $14 to $17 a share. However, investors are anticipating a breakout as the company is set to unveil a new product line. If all goes well, the company's stock will soar. As such, investors are looking to get in now before the stock takes off for the moon.

So, investors are prepared to get in now. However, there is no telling when the price will take off. Buying the stock now and waiting for it to take off would imply using the buy and hold strategy. However, investors are never willing to tie up their money for longer than absolutely necessary. Consequently, investors can use options to both buy and sell stocks.

In this example, an investor can use a combination of call and put options. For example, the investor can use a call option to buy the stock at $16 and sell at $20. But here's the tricky part. It is unclear when the stock will take off, and most importantly, it is not clear if the stock will take off at all.

A savvy speculator purchases the options contracts to ensure that they will hedge their position. That way, they won't commit their money without being sure of what will happen. If the stock doesn't take off, the investor doesn't have to exercise any of the options. If anything, they will simply lose the money on the premiums. This is a small change compared to getting wiped out on a downturn. However, if the deal goes as expected, the profits will easily offset the cost of the contracts.

This is the reason why speculators live and die by their options. Since they clearly understand the way that options work, they can leverage them to their advantage. Moreover, if you plan to plan the speculation game, then you must use options in your favor. Otherwise, using the buy and hold strategy on long shots will cause you to miss a lot of opportunities. It is worth noting that the buy and hold strategy is great for blue-chip stocks, that is, companies that are certain to perform at or beyond expectations. Since these stocks are highly coveted, you can be sure that you can sell them at any time. Thus, they are the closest thing you'll find to a sure bet. Anything that isn't considered as blue-chip would best be treated as a speculative investment. Therefore, options must become your go-to option.

Writing Contracts

Writing options contracts is an alternative best employed by seasoned traders. The reason for this is that writers must have stock and/or cash on hand. Writing options can be attractive for investors and traders as most contracts are often unused. This means that you can basically keep the premium contract holders pay. However, you cannot assume that the contract will go unused. You must always assume the contract will be used. That way, you need to be ready. Otherwise, you'll run into trouble.

There are two ways in which you can make money as an options writer. The first is to agree with another party beforehand. That way, you draft up the contract based on the specific agreement you have with the counterparty. This type of arrangement is quite common with exotic options. The second way is to write up a contract and put it out there. That way, other investors can come along and buy it from you. To make that work, you need to look for the right terms. Often that means making the contract attractive so that other traders find value in it.

For example, you are holding stock in a corporation. As such, you are looking to sell it. In that case, you can write a call option. A buyer that's interested in purchasing stock in that corporation will find it and buy the rights. If the premium you have assigned makes sense to the buyer, then you have a deal. If the buyer exercises the contract, then you make the transaction.

So, please bear in mind that when you write the contract, you don't have the right to exercise it. You sell that right to the other party. That's why you can't assume that it won't be exercised. You must always assume it will be.

Also, you can write a put option. In this case, you are looking to buy stock in a company. You write up the contract and then an interested party will buy the rights. That gives them the option to sell you the stock if they choose to. That means you must be ready to pay for the stock in case the contract is exercised.

Chapter 23: Options Strategies

The next thing we need to look at is some of the different strategies you can use when you want to trade-in options. Everyone needs to enter the market with some good strategies ahead of time. This makes it easier for them to make sure they enter the market at the right times, and that they can pick the right times to exit the market as well.

The Long Call

This is a strategy that bets the asset will rise above the strike price before the expiration date. If you look at the underlying asset and the market and you think the price will rise before the options contract ends, then the long call is a good one to use.

If you do this call well, then the upside on this call can provide you with an infinite number of profits until the expiration, as long as that asset sees an increase in the price. Even if you see that the stock is moving in the wrong way, it is possible to salvage at least part of the premium that you have by selling the call before it expires. The downside is a complete loss of the premium paid if the stock does not go up or if it starts to go down, but this is less risky than purchasing the stock outright.

The Long Put

The long put is going to be worth the most when you see the stock reaches $0 per share, so the maximal value will be the strike price times 100 times the number of contracts that you decide to do. You also get the benefit that if the price of the asset goes up, you can still sell the put and then save up some of the premium, as long as you still have a bit of time before your expiration. The most you can lose is all the loss of your premium based on how much you spend.

The reason that we want to use this one is that the long put is a good way to wager on the asset declining. If you can stomach that you may potentially lose the whole premium, you can do this one. If you do see a big decline in that asset, then you will earn more with the puts than you would by short selling that stock.

The Short Put

The short put is basically seen as the opposite of the long put. The investor will sell their put, or they will go short. With this one, the investor is betting that the stock will stay flat, or it will continue to rise until it reaches the expiration date. Remember that with this one, the other person is betting the price will go down and you hope it doesn't. Like the long call, this short put can be a wager on a stock rising, but it has some big differences that go along with it.

While a long call will bet that there will be a big increase in the value of a stock or other asset, the short put is going to be more modest and can pay off more modestly, though it can work in some situations.

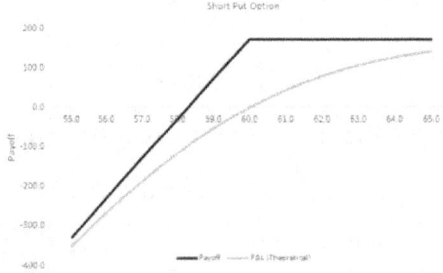

Covered Calls

The first thing that we want to look at is the covered call. This is a good strategy because it will help to reduce your risks of being all alone on a stock that is long while making sure you can get some income in the process.

The trade-off that we will get with this one is that you need to be willing to sell off the shares you have at a price that is set, which will be the short strike price. Not sticking with this will cause you to lose money in the process. To help you execute this one, you need to purchase the underlying stock on the options contract, just like we talked about before. Then at the same time, we need to write, or sell, one of the call options on that exact same share.

Married Put

We can then move on to the second type of strategy that we can use within our options, and this one is known as the married put. In this strategy, the investor will purchase an asset, such as some shares of a chosen stock. And then, at the same time, they will purchase the put options for the same number of shares in that same stock. The holder of the put option will then have the right to sell, within the time limits of the option, to sell the stock using that strike price, no matter what the value of the stock is all about.

The reason that you, as an investor, would use this one is that it can help to protect them against any downside risk when they hold onto the stock. Then this strategy will work just like an insurance policy and will help to establish the price floor if the price of the stock decides that it wants to turn and fall quickly.

Bull Call Spread

Now we can move on to a great strategy to learn about because it works well with options and in the stock market if you decide to purchase the stocks outright. With this strategy, known as the bull call, spread, the investor is going to buy calls of an asset at a specific strike price, and then at the same time they will also buy the same number of calls, but at a higher strike price. Both of these will come with the same asset, so don't try to do it with two different ones, and they will have the same expiration with them.

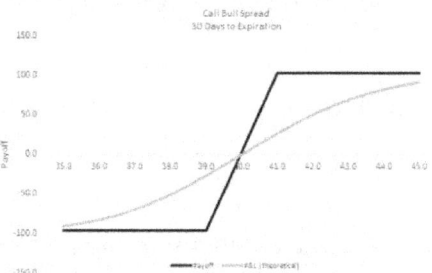

Bear Put Spread

We spent some time talking about the bull call spread and how to use it when we think the market is bullish. But there are times when the market will go in the opposite direction, and we will end up with a bearish market instead. This is why working with a bear put spread could be the best option to help you out here.

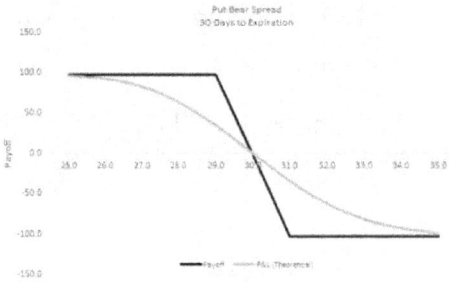

Protective Collar

Sometimes it is a good idea to find ways to protect yourself in the market. It would be nice if the stock market, or any other underlying asset that you use with options, would follow a pattern that made sense and always stayed the same. But if that happened, then everyone would get into the market, and you would not be able to make the money that you want. The good news is the protective collar strategy will be able to help you get this done, ensuring you are protected in the market.

The Long Straddle

You can't look much at the world of investing without looking at some of the straddle options that are out there. This is a great strategy that you can use that will provide you with lots of choices and can make it easier for you to stay protected and make as much money as possible. And we are going to spend some time looking at how to complete what is known as a long straddle.

The long straddle strategy will be one where the investor can purchase the put and the call option at the same time. You want to do this with the same asset underneath the option, with the same strike price and the same expiration date. Everything has to be the same on this one, except that you do one put option and one call option.

The Long Strangle

In the long strangle strategy, the investor will spend their time working on an out of the money call option, while also going through and doing an out of the money put option at the same time. We need to make sure the underlying asset of both is the same and that we keep the expiration date the same as well. This can help you to protect yourself if you are not certain which direction the market will go.

Long Call Butterfly Spread

This is a fun one that allows you to stay in the market a bit longer and can make it easier for you to really see some results with what you are doing here. However, we have to make sure that we use it well and that we are getting in and out at the right parts along the way. The strategy we will talk about here is known as a long call butterfly spread.

All of the other strategies we have taken a look at so far in this guidebook were a combination of two contracts or two positions. With this one, though, we will want to use the call options. With this one, the investor will combine both the bear spread and the bull spread strategies that were earlier in this guidebook. You would also need to make sure you work with three strike prices that are different. You will still stick with the same expiration date and the same underlying assets along the way to make this happen.

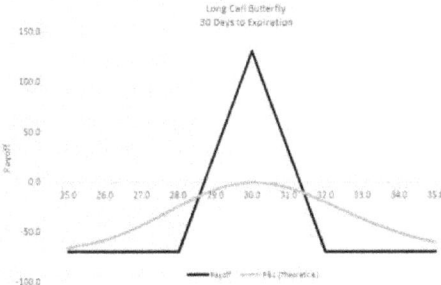

Iron Condor

The next choice that we are going to add to our list is known as the iron condor. This one is really interesting and allows us to work on a lot of different things at once to see some results.

The way to construct the iron condor is to sell one of your out of the money puts, and then we go through the process of selling one out of the money call while also buying one out of the money call, making sure we do this last one at a higher strike price.

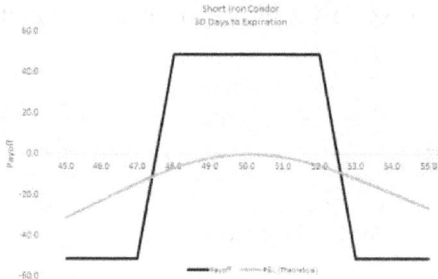

Iron Butterfly Strategy

Then it is time to move on to a strategy that is known as the iron butterfly strategy. We talked about the iron condor and the butterfly spread, so now we get to have some fun and work with the strategy of the iron butterfly. To make this one work, the investor will need to sell one of them at the money puts, and then they can buy an out of the money put, while also taking the time to sell one of them at the money calls and purchasing an out of the money call. This is a lot of steps, so make sure you really know the market and how it is supposed to work before you start.

Chapter 24: Successful Trading Tactics

One successful essential thing and another successful thing will lead to a successful outcome. Let's get acquainted with some of the ways we need to be exposed and consider how our options transactions can be successful.

Which Trade is Profitable?

There are several basic types of options trading that a novice and even experienced investors should know and master their options trading that will bring a lot of profit. Here are some of the cost-effective ways.

1. Buy to open. This requires the initiation of a new order to secure the new option and final improvement of the existing trading position, as assessed based on previous trading activities.

2. Sell to open. Selling for opening means selling a specific option that you do not necessarily have and eventually gaining a new position or an improved position in your options trading business.

3. Buying to close. This is buying a specific option that you previously sold on the market, and ultimately reducing your position in the options trading market.

4. Closed sale. In these types of transactions, an order is made to sell a specific option in which everything you sell has previously been bought and ultimately reduces or leaves the existing position in the transaction market.

How to Be a Thriving Option Investor

Below are some ways in which we can shine in this options trading field.

1. Risk management. Life itself is a risk, which means that risk will always be presented. The option trader must master all possible ways to minimize the number of risks that may arise and learn from each of them for proper future management. For example, in the capital sector, the entrepreneur should have an extensive plan with detailed information on the strict use of capital. Losses are also part of the consequences of trading options, and with poor capital handling,

everything can fall over. Think about how lousy market volatility can be, which leads to large amounts of capital and substantial losses.

2. Be the boss in numbers. Options trading involves extensive use of names. Do you know the implied volatility? Is money an option or not? For beginners who do not have a single trace of what is happening, kindly engage in in-depth research and try to pay attention. For brokers and experts, keep learning about the different numbers in options trading. Life stops when you stop learning.

3. They have great discipline. We encourage self-discipline when you engage in options trading. It is a driving force that will push you in line with the plan with so much determination. You can follow your specific plans and strategies, learn a lot from trading activities, and gain the right skills and experience to trade options more effectively. Remember that your plan strategies are the primary objects at this time.

4. Great patience. Every aspect of life is a process led by continuous growth. Trade during several market moves and learn from it. During these commercial travel options, you will be exposed to various situations that you need to learn and master. Find out about the potential risks, some market tricks, and so on. Well, get the best experience because it's always the best teacher.

5. Have your trading style. The intended trading style is usually used in the trading plan. Your trading style should be strictly followed and updated with new skills and information as you engage in various options transactions. Follow the program without any other impact and watch how you grow by trading options.

6. Trading plan. Unplanned planning for failure. This means that the loser will only be reflected if no planning occurs. Successful entrepreneurs have big plans. Great ideas include the right strategies, features, discussions, in-depth research, great self-discipline, goals, and reasonable goals. Establishing good trading plans is a clear reflection of the great success in options trading.

7. Emotionally stable. Emotions can be very distracting when we get involved in various aspects of our lives. Losing trade should be treated as a bad day, which is useful with good educational

experience and knowledge for a bright future. Winning days should also be a learning day, appreciating the right moves expressed that day.

8. Intensive learning and proactivity. Life always remains stagnant when you stop learning. Knowledge is good and evil, including master and learn every possible expressed move

Also, subscribe to a variety of channels and blogs to get the extensive knowledge you need in trading options. Learning allows you to inform and educate about actual trading activities that are usually involved in options trading.

9. Secure, accurate business records. We encourage you to learn from past mistakes and strategic development to become a successful options investor.

10. Determination and commitment. This entails a lot of thrusts that should rule a beginner or an experienced trader to get what is best for him in options trading and getting down learn some tips on how to succeed as an options trader.

11. be flexible. Another thing to add is that when you feel it, the market does not suit you at all during this particular period of options trading, find something constructive to do. Master every possible market move that will likely occur in options trading and master it.

12. Basic understanding and interpretation. The trader should be familiar with the necessary market terminology to understand the primary activities of the market and learn the different ways to start and handle options trading. The interpretation consists of the analysis of actual commercial transactions on the market and obtaining the necessary information in each of the commercial activities. This helps the investor always pay attention to the reality Market, not hype, depending on significant market terms.

13. be aggressive. Being aggressive in options trading means that there is a desire for great success, and the chances of getting big profits are so high. A dynamic option trader most often participates in in-depth scientific research, learning new and learning new lucrative trade moves. This gives the trader extensive experience and skills to face all kinds of risks that may be involved in the market, and in a short time, the trader accredited a great expert in options trading.

14. Emotionally stable. Different feelings on the market should not control an investor engaged in options trading. Lost days should not in any way discourage the trader from deciding to stay with the market hype. It is recommended that investors follow their plan and always stick to it down their different strategies.

15. Excellent choice of goods. The option trader must select the appropriate sell option. Weigh are you able to handle the right inventory and manage the necessary risks that are highly involved in them? Most importantly, will the shares benefit the investor in making large profits?

16. Good capital management. When money is important this comes to trade. Monitor and plan any amount of capital that you plan to use on the market. Always be careful with the amount of money you put into each option. Accepting losses is still an alternative when it comes to options trading, a failure that can knock you down and lead you to bankruptcy. Plan the capital that you plan to invest in the company.

17. Powerful trading platforms. The platform on which various commercial activities take place is essential in all types of involvement in option transactions. Your best platform should consist of fantastic navigation tools, learning sources, and other amazing features.

18. Selling options are most often preferred than buying options while practicing buying and selling strategies that ultimately help the investor to make a large amount of profit.

19. Correct time. As an entrepreneur, you should be informed about good and bad times. Enter the market when the time is quite favorable. Bad timing leads to significant losses in the options trading market, which leads to a substantial decline in finance.

Strategies That Are Successful in Options Trading

Good strategies set out in the options trading plan should be a priority.

Use the appropriate period. A longer period, for example, five years is recommended during in-depth research and analysis of various sources to establish good strategies. Remember to choose a fairly long period to get up-to-date information and to report it as part of learning.

Covered connection. This type of strategy includes both, trading in underlying shares and options contracts. The ultimate goal of a secured connection is to collect income through premiums and mainly sell inventory that you already own. Here are some ways to consider when creating a program connection:

Buy shares and buy in the form of shares. Sell a purchase contract for every 100 shares you own. Then wait for the connection to be made.

The risk associated with secured connections maintains a cautious inventory position that may fail over time. Large parts of the profits from this particular combination are equal to the price of the specified call option and the lower purchase price of the underlying shares.

We are introducing to the market. This strategy consists in the fact that the investor has made two purchases on the stock exchange and a put option. The advantage of this is that as an options investor, you can protect yourself against several losses. Launching is also considered beneficial when buying a security that has an optimistic attitude. The market launch strategy is also necessary to protect the depreciation, in particular of share prices.

Market sales are also called the synthetic long call because of the similarities in the number of potential profits on both sides.

Spread options. This strategy was established by selling several options and purchase options of the same class and from the same collateral with different exercise prices and expiry dates.

Butterfly spread. Butterfly includes four calls to buy and sell and is also considered a market-neutral strategy that can pay the majority of its underlying shares without worrying about expiration dates.

There are several varieties of butterfly spreads that usually use four types of options with three different strike prices. To add, different types of butterflies have different levels of maximum profit amount and maximum loss amount, which usually occur when trading options.

Chapter 25: Tips to Become a Successful Trader

As you must have understood by now, that in the world of the stock market, one of the most versatile financial instruments are options. You can boost your net profit by leveraging their versatility, but you also have to deal with the potential for loss despite all these advantages.

Every tip mentioned below is equally important, and only when you master all of them will you be able to produce a cumulative effect that will help in your future trades. Beginners are mostly in a hurry to know how they can maximize the profits, but they miss out on the more important details in between. Make a Trading Plan

A trading plan is something that every trader should have. It is a plan that will have all the specifics clearly written, and this includes your entry, exit, and also criteria for managing money in the best way possible. There is a myth in the market that trading comes naturally to some people, and thus, they do not need any trading plan, but this is so wrong. Trading is something that you have to learn – what comes naturally is your ability to work hard and learn something new. People might have an innate skill with numbers or identifying patterns, but even then, you have to learn the strategies and what should be used when. Some skills and traits cannot be built overnight and require experience.

If you ask any professional options trader, they will tell you how important it is to always work on building an in-depth base of knowledge and then find out your cognitive biases that hamper your decision-making skills. You can then figure out ways to fight your biases and overcome them. But all of this is possible only when you have a trading plan. You need not have the same trading plan month after month or year after year. Every month you might come across something new that can be incorporated into your plan. In that case, you can tweak your plan according to your newfound knowledge. But before you apply anything from your trading plan on a real-time trade, you must test it on the historical data that is available to you.

When you have a fixed strategy in place, you don't have to worry about when or what decisions you need to make. The entire process of decision-making becomes much more simplified. The trading plan will not only have all your goals clearly written but also the strategies you plan to undertake to fulfill those goals and the amount of risk you are comfortable taking in the process. According to experts, you should try keeping a maximum of only 1% of your total account at risk in a single trade. Another important thing to keep in mind while designing your trading plan is that it should clearly point out where you are going to enter a trade and when you are going to do that; you should also mention the possible indicators that will signal you and similarly, you also need to have a fixed exit point.

But the key point here is that even when you have a trading plan, you have to promise yourself that you will stick to the plan no matter what. Some people deviate from it far too much and make trades outside the plan, which only causes even more loss.

Start Thinking of Trading Like a Business

If you want to be a successful trader, you cannot take it lightly; you have to treat trading as if you are running a business. It shouldn't be a hobby. The difference is that when you are approaching the subject as a hobby, you don't really feel obligated to learn new things or improve your skillset, which is important to be successful. Also, if you treat it like a job, then after a certain point of time, you will only be thinking of the paycheck and otherwise get frustrated. Thus, trading should be treated more like a business where you are going to have to pay taxes, incur losses and expenses, handle risk, and overcome stress. When you start trading, consider yourself as a small business owner, and then with proper planning and strategizing, you can upgrade your business to the next level.

If you are wondering as to in what other ways can you treat trading like your business, then here is what else you can do –

- Have a Vision – Just like you have a vision for your business; it is important to have it for trading too. But if you don't know how to, then think about why you started options trading in the first place, and from there, it would be easier for you to find your vision. Once you have figured out your vision, print or write it in bold letters on a paper and then hang it somewhere where you can spot it easily throughout the day.
- Have Proper Funding – You need to keep trading funds ready before you jump into the market. In today's world, you can start trading with as low as $50 or $100, but even

though that will get you started, will it be enough to sustain you in the long term? If you want to be in the market for a long time, then proper funding is necessary. Thus, prepare your starting capital.

- Always Think Long-Term – When you are strategizing your trades or thinking of anything related to options trading, think about what you are going to do in the long-term.

- Prepare a Daily Trading Routine – You need to be disciplined to be a successful options trader. And one of the most important things to do is to have a daily trading routine. This means you will set a time every day when you will analyze the market and when you are going to stop trades as well. Also, your routine should perfectly match your everyday lifestyle. It shouldn't seem like a burden.

Maintain a Trading Journal

A trading journal is a very powerful tool and something that every trader should have to be successful. It also instills in you the art of discipline. It is not anything fancy but just a written record of all the trades that you are making and what happened when you made the trade. Some things worth noting are market conditions, expiration time, size of the trade, notes on your emotions during the trade, and whether the trade was a successful one. The entries might not be the same for everyone. The entries should be customized based on your trading style so that it suits your ways.

I know what you might be thinking – keeping a trading journal is time-consuming and tedious. Even if it is so, when you maintain a trading journal, it helps you become disciplined and consistent at what you are doing. In the long run, both these qualities will help you a lot in the world of trading.

So, make sure you note down the patterns and charts you are watching and how your trade has been impacted by certain events. When you keep noting these things down over a certain period, you will be able to spot your mistakes and then work on rectifying them. For example, a trading journal often helps option traders figure out whether it was too early for them to exit the trade or whether they fell into the trap of a false signal.

When you have a detailed record of everything that you did, it helps in coming up with better strategies. In fact, this is why noting down your emotions is essential. This will help you understand whether you have a pattern of allowing your emotions to affect your trade.

Moreover, the journal will help you monitor your progress over a while. You should also write down your trading goals in the journal because often, writing down your goals is what helps you or gives you the extra push in achieving them. With time, you will understand how the trading journal can boost your confidence. And when you realize the benefits, it will no longer seem like a chore.

Make the Best Use of Technology

There is a lot of competition in trading, and you have to make this assumption that the person who is on the other side of the trade has access to the latest technology and is making the best use of it too.

Today, you can get access to plenty of charting platforms and other tools that will help you perform an in-depth analysis of the market conditions, and there are infinite ways in which you can view the market with the help of these tools. If you do not take the help of these things, you might make some wrong decisions that would turn out to be way more costly than you'd ever imagine. There is plenty of historical data available on these platforms that you can use for backtesting your strategies. In fact, some of these platforms will also give you the option of receiving real-time updates on your smartphone so that you can stay notified about everything that is happening on the market even on-the-go and keep monitoring your trades.

So, if you have been taking this technology for granted all this time, you need to gear up and make the best use of it because others are already going ahead of you. Once you start using these technological advantages, you will be able to see for yourself how your trading performance enhances drastically. You will stay current with every new product that launches and realize your hard work's proper rewards.

Understand Yourself

Did you know that before you start trading, it is very important to understand yourself, and sometimes it is even more important than understanding the market? Yes, there is no need to shy away from this because to become successful in options trading, a little bit of introspection into who you are is of utmost importance. You will be able to study your biases and figure out what you can do to overcome them. Strategizing your trades is one thing and understanding your mind and your emotions that affect those trades is a completely different thing altogether.

In Chapter 6, we have already spoken at length as to how you can keep your emotions in check while trading so that they do not affect your trading decisions. In fact, sometimes, all you need to do is maintain a positive attitude, and you will easily be able to spot the profitable trading opportunities that come your way. Be realistic while examining yourself and see whether you possess the qualities required to be a successful trader. If not, then there is no need to beat yourself up for it. Own your shortcomings and start working on them from today.

You also need to judge your abilities to manage things and regulate your emotions when it comes to an uncertain condition. No matter how much chaos there is, a successful trader can look past all of that and make the right decision.

You need to be able to evaluate risks instantly and determine what you need to do to minimize those risks and maximize your profits.

Make Peace with Losing a Trade

You have to understand that no matter how successful you are, there will be some trades that you cannot win. So, when you see that things are not working your way and the market is going in the opposite direction to what you predicted, you have to make yourself understand that you need to get out of the trade before your losses start escalating even more. This is what trading discipline is all about. No matter how disastrous things have become, you have to learn to take your losses and step out. Every loss that you encounter in the market will teach you something, and you must learn the lesson and promise yourself not to repeat the same mistake.

If you speak with any successful trader, you will realize that they have faced failures too, but they did not let their failures determine their life course. So, you shouldn't let your failures make you feel bad or lay you low. A part of trading is owning your losses. But the key factor is ensuring that your total gains are always more than your total losses.

Avoid Buying Options that Are Out-of-the-Money

This is because if we are to follow statistics, then these types of options have proven to be the least profitable. To overcome time decay, the price of the stock will have to move in your favor, and that has to be fast enough. Don't ever forget that options are decaying assets. That is why it is advised that you sell options that are out-of-the-money and not buy them.

Be Patient

Patience is a very important virtue that is necessary for traders. You cannot become a successful trader in a day. If you are a beginner who only started trading recently, then your first couple of years are going to be about learning different things about the market, and the learning curve is going to be quite steep. With time, as you get exposed to the different conditions of the market, you will keep learning more. And even if you make a mistake, note it down so that even if that market condition returns, you know what not to do. Sometimes, it is even more important to stay patient and not to do anything to make your trade successful.

If you become impatient and you exit a trade before it's time or enter a trader too late, you might lose a lot of potential profit. That is why having a clear idea of the trading strategy is very important so that your bottom line is not affected by rookie moves.

Another meaning of having patience is that even if you faced huge losses, you would not give in to the urge to do revenge trading and use the loss as an opportunity to brush up on your basics and then gain a better understanding of the situation.

These were some of the most important tips to keep in mind if you want to be a successful trader. But apart from this, there is one more thing that I would like to remind you – always stay updated with the news of the day and don't believe everything right off the bat. You need to be able to differentiate between reality and the hype and understand what a promising piece of news for your trading strategy might be.

Conclusion

When it comes to trading options, there's a lot of different options that you can choose from when it comes to your approach. Options are a great way to make money in the stock market. A lot of people don't understand options trading, and they think that it's too complicated. That's not true. For most people, options trading is the best way to make money on the stock market.

Options trading is a great way to gain exposure for your company, learn the ins and outs of options trading, and make a little extra money. Options trading is a great example of how simple it can be to make money. In options trading, you sell an option contract to buy or sell a certain quantity of something at a set price within a certain period. In conclusion, options trading is a great way to make money quickly without putting in huge amounts of time and effort. Every beginner should start by buying cheap puts and calls on stocks that they already have an interest in.

The most important thing about options trading is to make sure that you're getting the best possible price on your options. Options trading is a great way to make money if you're willing to learn about the options and know what they are. Options trading is about making decisions at the right time. It's important to be prepared for each situation to ensure you're able to make good decisions on what you want to do in a trade.

Options trading is a great way to make money, but it's also one of the riskiest investments you could make. Being an options trader can be really fun and exciting. However, it can also be dangerous if you don't understand the basics of options trading. These basics can help you make more informed decisions about your trades and protect yourself from taking unnecessary risks. This is an area of finance that may be new to you, but it's a great way to make money. Options trading is pretty simple, you buy a call option on an asset and people can only sell it to you.

Options are one of the most complicated investment vehicles to understand and invest in. If you don't understand how options work, then you're going to end up losing a lot of money. Options are a great way to diversify your investment portfolio. If you're trading options, don't just look at the stock price when you make a decision. There are many different kinds of options trading, but the most common type is covered calls. For this kind of trade, a trader can buy a call option with an expiration date as far out as the trader chooses.

Options trading is a way to speculate on the market but it's important to know the risks involved when you're making this type of investment. Options are a form of derivatives, which are contracts that derive their value from underlying assets. The options you trade will be based on some underlying asset such as shares, bonds, commodities, currencies, or indices. This is a very simple strategy that anyone can do. If you want to be able to buy or sell options, you have to be able to identify when they're reasonably priced.

www.ingramcontent.com/pod-product-compliance
Lightning Source LLC
Chambersburg PA
CBHW080833220526
45467CB00008B/2263